On the Beauty of Women

On the Beauty of Women

Agnolo Firenzuola

Translated and edited by
KONRAD EISENBICHLER
and JACQUELINE MURRAY

upp

University of Pennsylvania Press

Philadelphia

Frontispiece: Titian, *Flora* (Florence: Uffizi). Courtesy of Alinari/Art Resource, NY.

Copyright © 1992 by the University of Pennsylvania Press
All rights reserved
Printed in the United States of America

Library of Congress Cataloging-in-Publication Data

Firenzuola, Agnolo, 1493–1543.
 [Discorsi delle bellezze delle donne. English]
 On the beauty of women / Agnolo Firenzuola; translated and edited by Konrad
Eisenbichler and Jacqueline Murray.
     p.   cm.
 Fictional dialogues.
 Translation of: Discorsi delle bellezze delle donne.
 Includes bibliographical references and index.
 ISBN 0-8122-3158-9. — ISBN 0-8122-1404-8 (pbk.)
 I. Eisenbichler, Konrad.   II. Murray, Jacqueline.   III. Title.
PQ4622.D5713   1992
853'.3—dc20   92-21836
                                                              CIP

for our mothers
Ivetta Eisenbichler
Louise Murray

Contents

Illustrations

Acknowledgments

We would like to express our appreciation to Mara Ezerkalns Vilčinskas for her careful reading of our work and for her generous advice. We are also grateful to the two anonymous readers for the University of Pennsylvania Press, whose enthusiasm for our project and constructive criticism were equally helpful. And we thank the Thomas Fisher Rare Book Library, Dr. Richard Landon, Director, for permission to photograph and reproduce in this volume the illustrations from their copy of the 1562 Giunti edition.

Much of the work on this translation was carried out while Jacqueline Murray held a Canada Research Fellowship from the Social Sciences and Humanities Research Council of Canada and a Senior Fellowship at the Centre for Reformation and Renaissance Studies, and while Konrad Eisenbichler enjoyed a sabbatical leave from Victoria University (University of Toronto).

We would like to thank the three readers and four organizations for they have, in their different ways, contributed much to the successful conclusion of the project. The support of innumerable colleagues and friends at Toronto and Windsor facilitated the completion of our work. To them, too, we owe our thanks.

K.E.
J.M.

Introduction

Biography

Agnolo Firenzuola was born in Florence on 28 September 1493. His father Bastiano, following in the family tradition, worked as a notary. His mother Lucrezia was the daughter of Alessandro Braccesi, a mid-rank humanist employed as secretary of the Florentine republic and ambassador to Siena. Bastiano Firenzuola's quiet career allowed him to raise his large family without experiencing serious repercussions from the political turmoil of Florentine politics. Although Alessandro Braccesi, who had been closely affiliated with the Savonarolan party, suffered a permanent political setback when Savonarola was ousted and executed, Bastiano Firenzuola displayed a keen sense of bourgeois adaptability and was able to continue his notarial career, working in particular for the Vallambrosian order. Agnolo, his firstborn son, received the fundamentals of a humanist education in Florence. At the age of sixteen, Agnolo was sent to study law, first in Siena (1509–1516) and then in Perugia (1516–1518), to prepare for a notarial career in the footsteps of his father and grandfather.

As was the case with many other Italian writers (Petrarch, for one), the legal career forced upon the young man by family rather than personal inclination did not hold Agnolo's full attention. Indeed, Firenzuola wrote with unconcealed bitterness of the years he spent "with great effort and without any pleasure [pursuing the study of] the ill-served laws [in the] most noble and lively city of Siena."[1] It comes as no surprise, then, that Firenzuola's university years were spent more in the company of other carefree and boisterous youths than in the pursuit of legal studies. His friend and fellow reveler, the scurrilous writer Pietro Aretino (1492–1556), recalled their student escapades in Perugia in a letter of 26 October 1541:

> Who is not moved when he remembers the noble progress of your conversation? For you grant joyful pleasure to the spirit of those who are on friendly terms with you—as I was, when you were a student in Perugia, a man in Florence, and a prelate in Rome. . . . And certainly I often recall the pleasant escapades of our youth. Do not think I have forgotten how that old woman

ran away frightened and disappeared from sight when, in broad daylight, you told her off from your window. You were wearing only your shirt, and I was naked. The fight at Camilla Pisana's house is still in my mind, that time you left me to entertain her. And as I remember that, I still see Bagnacavallo, looking at me speechless. But his looks and his silence at the overturned table were saying loud and clear: "That man deserves the worst." And as I remember this I hear Giustiniano Nelli, God bless his soul, fall on the ground in sheer delight at all the clamor, as I fell on the ground at the pain of hearing of his death at Piombino, a loss to all of Italy, not just Siena.[2]

In two of his later sonnets Firenzuola himself remembers the beautiful women of Siena and the carefree years of his youth spent in courting them.[3]

After finally graduating in law from the University of Perugia (1518), Agnolo entered monastic life in the Vallambrosian order. This was not the result of a deeply felt spirituality, but rather the inevitable conclusion to a well-planned family strategy. Agnolo's father Bastiano had seen his father-in-law's promising career as a civil servant to the Florentine republic cut short by the vicissitudes of factional civic politics, while his own career as a notary for the Vallambrosian order had survived the turmoil. With experience such as this, it seemed advisable that Bastiano place his well-educated son in a career that would offer him both stability and scope. Although it was unusual for a firstborn son to join a monastic order, the Church provided such an opportunity.

This "vow of convenience" led Firenzuola to Rome (1518), where his legal training was placed at the service of the Vallambrosian order as its appointed Roman attorney (*procuratore*). In the elegant city of Pope Leo X, Firenzuola, still not interested in the law, devoted his time to literary and social interests. He frequented the papal court, the patrician palaces of nobles and prelates, and the Roman Academy. He moved in a circle of friends and acquaintances that included not only Pietro Aretino, his friend from university years, but also the courtier and comic poet Francesco Berni (1497/8–1535); the poet and rogue Francesco Maria Molza (1489–1544); the scholar, historian, and future bishop Paolo Giovio (1483–1552); the poet, writer, diplomat, and future archbishop Giovanni Della Casa (1503–1556); and many others.

In Rome Firenzuola obtained the minor ecclesiastical benefices that financed his worldly and literary interests. He also began to write. In 1524 he composed a treatise on orthography, *The Expulsion of the New Letters Unnecessarily Added to the Tuscan Language* (*Discacciamento delle nuove lettere inutilmente aggiunte nella lingua toscana*), in which he argued, often in a comic vein, against the proposed introduction into the Italian alphabet of several letters from the Greek. This mock-linguistic work marks the point where he began to attain a certain amount of fame and prestige in Roman literary circles. In the letter of 1541 mentioned above, Aretino recalled how Pope Clement VII had been impressed by Firenzuola's treatise and how, together with Monsignor Pietro Bembo,[4] the pope had asked to meet the young writer: "I still laugh at the pleasure Pope Clement had the night I led him to read what you had written about Trissino's omegas. Because of that piece His Holiness, together with Monsignor Bembo, asked to meet you personally."[5] In the introduction to the dialogue *On the Beauty of Women,* Firenzuola proudly recounted this moment of glory, saying the pope chose to read the treatise and the "First Day" of his collection of short stories (*Ragionamenti*) himself, out loud, in front of "the best minds of Italy" (p. 4).

Such renown, however, was neither notable nor long-lasting. In the fast-paced cosmopolitan world of Medicean Rome, Firenzuola was easily and often eclipsed by the keen minds and lively wits that adorned the papal and patrician courts. His assorted love poetry, his collection of short stories (*Ragionamenti d'amore*), and his translation of Apuleius's *The Golden Ass,* all written under the inspiration of an unidentified woman whom he calls Costanza Amaretta ("Bitter Constancy"), failed to ensure Firenzuola's fame and prestige. Disappointed by the lukewarm success his works had achieved, saddened by the sudden death of Costanza (1525), and debilitated by syphilis, Firenzuola received dispensation from his monastic vows (4 May 1526) and retired from social and public circles.

There is little biographical information on Firenzuola for the period 1526–1538, years which seem to have been spent primarily in a strenuous effort to cure himself of syphilis and regain his strength. It seems he remained in Rome until at least 1530, and possibly until 1534, when Clement VII, his patron, died. He was in Florence in 1530, and may have settled there between 1535 and 1538. The information is sketchy and uncertain.[6]

Firenzuola reappeared in 1538 in Prato, once more a Vallambrosian monk and now abbot of the monastery of San Salvatore a Vaiano. The last five years of his life were spent in Prato, in the comfort of his abbey and in the certain knowledge that in this provincial town he could at last fulfull his dream of social and literary fame. It was at this time that Firenzuola, after a long silence, began seriously to write again. He wrote the dialogue *On the Beauty of Women,* the *First Version of the Animals' Discourses,* and his two comedies (*The Triple Marriage* and *The Ludici*). He also claimed to have translated Horace's *Ars poetica*,[7] but if he did so the work is no longer extant. His literary production and the friendship and patronage of the most eminent families of Prato, especially the Buonamici, granted him an important role in the cultural life of the town. He was, for example, one of the founding members of the learned academy of the Addiaccio.[8]

But even in this provincial milieu Firenzuola eventually floundered and managed to alienate himself from the social elite he had sought so much to impress. He quarreled with friends, withdrew from the Addiaccio, and founded a rival academy, the Secondo Addiaccio. His ecclesiastical benefice of San Salvatore was withdrawn, and he was reduced to being a mere boarder at the abbey. In the last few months of his life Firenzuola suffered the social ostracism he had brought on himself. His troubles were compounded by personal financial difficulties and a legal squabble with his siblings over matters pertaining to their father's estate. He died suddenly and alone on 27 or 28 June 1543. His next of kin were not notified until nearly two weeks later. The family rift and his personal finances were such that his heirs refused to accept the small inheritance he had left, claiming it was "more useless and damaging than useful and profitable."[9]

The unhappy circumstances of Firenzuola's last months and his complete rejection by family and friends are counterbalanced by the posthumous success of his works. Some not only underwent several editions and enjoyed critical attention, but were also translated into French.

Firenzuola's Works

Of all his literary works, only the *Expulsion of the New Letters* was printed during Firenzuola's lifetime (1524). It is a mock-linguistic disputation against Gian Giorgio Trissino's proposal to introduce several Greek letters into the Italian alphabet. Although the treatise is more an amusing literary diversion than a serious work on orthography, it does reflect Firenzuola's involvement in contemporary discussions on language.

The debate over what constituted appropriate and correct Italian was at the forefront of literary and linguistic discussion in the sixteenth century and divided participants into different camps. The leader of the first was the Venetian Pietro Bembo (1470–1547), cardinal, poet, aesthete, and arbiter of taste, who claimed that contemporary Italians ought to imitate the vernacular of the great fourteenth-century writers. He thus proposed Petrarch's language and style as the canonical model for poetry and Boccaccio's language and style for prose.[10]

In proposing such a return to the language of the two major Florentine writers of the fourteenth century, Bembo and the *bembisti,* as his
followers were called, incurred the objections of modernists who argued
for the creation of a refined, contemporary vernacular Italian, not the
slavish imitation of long-dead writers. The modernists themselves, however, were divided into two further groups. The first, composed primarily
of Tuscans, agreed theoretically with Bembo in proposing a Florentine
model but differed practically from him in selecting the living language of
contemporary Florence. The historian and political theorist Niccolò Ma-
chiavelli, the prelate and theorist of good manners Giovanni Della Casa,
and Firenzuola himself are to be numbered among them. The second
group, composed primarily of non-Tuscans, proposed as a model an inter-
national, standardized, refined vernacular which, though based on the
Tuscan example, would be spoken and understood in all the courts and
capitals of the Italian peninsula. This group of writers included the courtier
Baldassare Castiglione.[11] Their spiritual father was, ironically, Dante Ali-
ghieri, who two centuries earlier in his treatise on the vernacular language
had proposed the creation of an Italian language that was, in his words,
"illustrious, pivotal, princely, and courtly."[12]

Firenzuola's writings reflect his commitment to contemporary Tuscan
vernacular. During his lifetime they enjoyed wide circulation in manuscript; soon after his death they were printed both in Florence and Venice,
the two major publishing centers in contemporary Italy.

The eight short stories comprising Firenzuola's *Discourses on Love,*
begun in 1523/24, never reached his intended number of thirty-six. The
tales, narrated by a carefree group of six young storytellers, are set in a
Boccaccian frame that is evident in the collection's structure but not its
language and style. Refusing to espouse Cardinal Pietro Bembo's proposal
that standard Italian should emulate the language of Boccaccio for prose
and Petrarch for poetry, Firenzuola wrote his stories in the freer, more
flowing mode of contemporary spoken Tuscan.

The translation of Apuleius's *Golden Ass,* completed in 1525, is better
termed a paraphrase than a translation. Firenzuola altered the original
significantly by casting himself in the role of Lucius and transferring the
story's setting to Italy. In so doing Firenzuola adhered to general Renaissance translation theories which deemed it perfectly acceptable to modify
the original in order to make it more palatable to current tastes. His
contemporaries concurred. They credited Firenzuola with enlivening the
tale, and the translation received both critical success and numerous print-
ings.

The *First Version of the Animals' Discourses,* completed in 1541, is a collection of fables much indebted to Aesop and to the Spanish adaptation of the Indian *Panchatantra* (1493). As the subtitle of the work clearly states, it retells the "civilized discourses in which animals, speaking marvelously and with beautiful style among themselves, narrate symbolic events, warnings, tales, proverbs, and witty remarks that teach how to live in society and how to govern others prudently." It enjoyed a wide circulation and was twice translated into French in the sixteenth century.

The Triple Marriage and *The Lucidi,* also composed in 1541, are prose comedies which, in their structure, plot, and language, are fully entrenched in the genre of sixteenth-century Italian erudite theatre. The first has a novelistic plot borrowed from Cardinal Bibbiena's play *Calandria,* while the second takes its plot and many of its lines and witticisms from Plautus's *Menaechmi.* Both were performed in Prato at Carnival time.

Among his epistolary writings the "Letter in Praise of Women" has a special importance for our topic. Firenzuola composed it to persuade his misogynist friend Claudio Tolomei not only that there had been great women in Antiquity, but also that they had been highly praised and esteemed by classical writers.[13] Tolomei had objected to Firenzuola's inclusion of women as participants in the discussions that formed the narrative frame for the *First Version of the Animals' Discourses,* saying that women should rather concern themselves "with determining how many hanks of wool it takes to make a piece of cloth."[14] Firenzuola responded that women, from Antiquity to the present time, had often participated and distinguished themselves in both discourse and literature. He further noted that women, too, can exemplify virtue, and illustrated each of the virtues by drawing on the example of women in Antiquity. In many ways Firenzuola's letter is merely another version of the catalogue of female worthies best illustrated by Boccaccio's *De claris mulieribus.* By its very traditional list of famous women, however, it draws our attention to the innovative approach and subject matter of the dialogue *On the Beauty of Women.*

On the Beauty of Women, completed in early 1541, moves away from the catalogue of moral-historical examples of female worthies and examines instead what constitutes feminine beauty and, by extension, virtue. The work recounts two conversations touching on women, beauty, balance, elegance, and style. It enjoyed significant critical success. There were several Italian editions in the sixteenth century and a French translation in 1578. It remains to this day an important document on the aesthetics and culture of sixteenth-century Italy.

The Structure of the Dialogue

On the Beauty of Women is set in the form of a Renaissance dialogue in which the author expresses his views on the subject by casting them in the context of a pleasant conversation among a group of friends. Although the genre found its origin and inspiration in the Platonic dialogues, it thrived on the immediacy of its characters, language, setting, and concerns. Unlike Renaissance learned comedy, for example, which borrowed characters, settings, and even plots from its Plauto-Terentian model, Renaissance dialogue was firmly grounded in the present and delved directly into questions of topical relevance. Frequent references to classical authors, science, and beliefs are presented merely as background information; the parameters and conclusions remain contemporary.

The work, then, claims to be a record of two conversations held by the young gentleman, Celso, and four ladies of Prato. The fictional dialogue is set within a frame composed of specific, identifiable surroundings, a group of contemporary characters, and the author's claim to have recorded from memory the words spoken by the participants. The piece is neither a direct transcription of the conversations nor the summary provided by one of the participants; rather, it is the calm, considered, literary product of a third party, the author, to whom one of the participants, Celso, has retold the particulars of the discussion. It is thus a "work of art" at two removes from reality—a copy of a copy. In Neoplatonic terms, it is an image of an image: Art reflecting Nature reflecting Idea.

In many ways the "frame," or narrative context into which the dialogue is set, is reminiscent of Boccaccio's frame for the *Decameron*. The discussions, for example, are carried out by a group of men and women who closely resemble Boccaccio's carefree gathering (*lieta brigata*). Although the numbers differ—Firenzuola's group consists of one man and four women, while Boccaccio's consists of three men and seven women—the total number of speakers in both groups has allegorical overtones. Firenzuola's five interlocutors may reflect the five elements, while Boccaccio's ten may be a reference to the notion that ten was a combination of the perfect numbers three and seven. The interpretative possibilities are myriad.

There are other noteworthy similarities. Firenzuola's first dialogue is set in a pleasant garden where the participants while away the afternoon under the shade of laurel and cypress trees, thus calling to mind the shady gardens to which Boccaccio's narrators retire in the afternoon to seek refuge from the heat and tell their tales. And although the Abbey of Grignano is not, like the villas on the hillside of Fiesole, on elevated ground, it does have a hill or mound where the carefree group gathers. The abbey, like the villas, is thus a place set apart, an idyllic space where the cares and worries of the city are forgotten, left behind at the city gates.

There are, however, significant differences between the two settings. First and foremost is the reason for the characters' presence in such an idyllic space. Boccaccio's youths had fled to the hillside of Fiesole to escape the Black Death that was decimating the population of Florence. Firenzuola's, on the other hand, were on a summer outing. Boccaccio's three gentlemen had come upon the seven ladies attending divine services in the church of Santa Maria Novella and worrying about their situation in that time of pestilence. Firenzuola's Celso found the women in the abbey's garden chatting idly about another's appearance. And while Boccaccio's youths move from one pleasant villa to the next, from one restful garden to the next, in a sequence of idyllic but identical places, Firenzuola's group moves but once, from a bucolic garden setting to a festive hall.

Each of the two conversations in Firenzuola's work is thus framed, or contextualized, differently. The first is set on a summer afternoon in the open air, on a small hilltop in the garden of the former Abbey of Grignano, under the shade of cypress and laurel trees. The second is set some days later, at the house of the elder of the ladies, during an evening family party hosted by her husband. The two settings are indicative of the different concerns of the two dialogues. The first, in the peacefulness of an afternoon in the garden, considers universal beauty as the proper, natural balance of individually beautiful parts. The second, in the festive excitement of a *soirée,* seeks to create a picture of perfect beauty by artificially combining the different "beautiful parts" available to the "creator." The standards of beauty established in the pastoral tranquility of the garden give life to the artistic, creative imagination of the human spirit. The movement from garden to hall, from nature to society, echoes the movement from Nature to Art, from divinely created beauty to humanly created beauty.

From an intellectual consideration of conventional standards of beauty and proportion, the dialogue thus moves to the practical sphere of artistic creation. That is, it moves from a conceptualization of ideal beauty to the actualization of such beauty in a specific beautiful woman. Ironically, as the participants in the discussion move from the theoretical to the practical, they realize that the product of their creative process, the beautiful woman *par excellence,* is a *chimera,* a reality that exists only in the creative imagination, an Idea.

The Characters of the Dialogue

The characters themselves reflect a sense of structure and proportion. The four women are evenly arranged into two older and two younger, two married and two unmarried—Mona Lampiada and Mona Amorrorisca on one side, Selvaggia and Verdespina on the other. Celso, an unmarried young man, is the fifth participant in the conversation. Before his appearance the women's discussion on beauty had been circular, not leading to any agreement or true understanding of the question. With his arrival and participation, the discussion acquires direction and, eventually, resolves itself.

In line with Renaissance cosmology and physiology, the four women can be seen as the four elements of the natural world—earth, air, fire, and water—while Celso is the fifth or quintessential element, the ether of the celestial spheres that revolve above the sublunar world. Selvaggia is easily identifiable with fire: warm and dry, with a choleric, assertive temperament. Mona Lampiada, on the other hand, is identifiable with the earth: cold and dry, with a melancholic, intellectual nature. Verdespina is air: warm and wet, with a sanguine, bright temperament. Finally, Mona Amorrorisca is water: cold and wet, and hence phlegmatic, or calm. Their respective humors associate them with the four seasons: Verdespina is spring, warm and wet; Selvaggia is summer, warm and dry; Mona Amorrorisca is autumn, cold and wet; and Mona Lampiada winter, cold and dry. The parallels continue with their ages: as spring is the first season, so Verdespina is the youngest and most lively of the group; and as winter marks the end of the cycle, so Mona Lampiada appears to be the eldest and most intellectually developed of the four women.

Given that the names of the participants are fictional, they lend themselves to metaphorical interpretation. Celso, by virtue of the Latin derivation of his name (*celsus,* meaning "high," "lofty"), is the one who controls and directs the conversation. He is also the loftiest of the five elements. Selvaggia is "the wild one," whom Celso wants but is unable to tame. He seems incapable of winning her over, and thus she remains "undomesticated." Verdespina, "green thorn," is the youngest and most innocent, the "greenest" of the four ladies. Amorrorisca (possibly from the Italian *ammorire,* "to become dark, tanned") may represent the experience of adulthood. Lampiada may draw her name either from the Greek and Latin *lampadias,* meaning "a comet resembling a blazing torch," or from Lampia, the name of a town in Arcadia.

In his introduction, Firenzuola clearly states that "the names and surnames . . . were chosen by chance [but] if someone were to unravel their fictitious names very carefully, we would find their real names covered with a thin veil" (p. 4). The attempt at unraveling the fiction behind the names has identified the character of Selvaggia with Selvaggia Rocchi, that of Mona Lampiada with her sister Clemenza, Mona Amorrorisca probably with a woman of the Gherardacci-Bocchineri family, and Verdespina with Smeralda Buonamici—the last two sisters-in-law of Selvaggia and Clemenza.[15] The four women are then related among themselves. Vannozzo Rocchi, father to Selvaggia and Clemenza, was a friend of Firenzuola and the tenant of the Abbey of Grignano, where the first dialogue took place. Clemenza was married to Pietro Buonamici, whose house was the setting for the second dialogue. The character of Celso, of course, is to be identified with the author himself. As Castiglione had paid homage to his hosts by setting his dialogues on the ideal courtier at the court of Urbino and within the learned, aristocratic circle around the Duchess Elisabetta Gonzaga, so Firenzuola paid homage to his friend Vannozzo Rocchi by contextualizing his dialogues on the beauty of women in a setting and with characters drawn from Vannozzo's family.

The identification of the characters and the ensuing appreciation of family connections between them does not, however, contribute significantly to our understanding of *On the Beauty of Women*. The nature of Renaissance dialogues was such that the participants, whether drawn from life or not, remained fictionalized persons within a literary genre. For this reason Firenzuola chided the unnamed woman who insisted on identifying him with the fictional Celso and said that if she "had done a little more reading, she would have come to appreciate the customary form of dialogues" (p. 6). Other writers of dialogues, from Plato to Castiglione, had employed the same technique of using historical persons as participants in their fictional conversations. The technique allowed the author to convey an aura of reality to an otherwise imaginary story and, in some cases, to strengthen a specific argument by placing it in the mouth of a particularly esteemed person. Such was the case in Castiglione's *Book of the Courtier,* where the discussion of beauty and Platonic love was led by none other than Cardinal Pietro Bembo, the contemporary authority on both subjects. In Thomas More's *Utopia,* on the other hand, the interlocutors are a mixed group of the historical (Peter Giles and Thomas More) and the fictional (Raphael Hythloday). In this work it is the fictional character who expounds on the geography and customs of the state of Utopia, possibly as an indication that such a country, like the man who describes it, exists only in the author's imagination. Along the same lines, in Firenzuola's dialogue, Celso expounds on beauty and creates an ideal woman who, like Celso "the lofty one," exists only within the higher reaches of human imagination.

The Courtship Game

Within the context of the dialogue a number of subjects and issues not specifically related to the topic under discussion are brought into play. The characters' personalities and their interrelationships inform and animate the discussion. Celso's feelings toward Selvaggia and her reaction, for example, provide a lively and at times saucy undercurrent to the conversation. When his eyes fall on her bosom, she rearranges her veil, partly from modesty and partly to tease him. And although she claims disinterest in his attention, she falls prey to jealousy when Celso praises the physical beauty of another young woman (p. 34).

The interaction between Selvaggia and Celso is structured along the lines of traditional courtly love as introduced into Italian love theory by the late medieval poetic school of the "Sweet New Style" (*Dolce stil nuovo*). Selvaggia's name, in fact, is a subtle clue to such an antecedent, for it repeats the name of Cino da Pistoia's beloved.[16] The allusion is more than a simple literary echo, for it not only points to the existence of a poetic antecedent, but also suggests a parallel between the nature of Cino's and Celso's relationship with their beloveds. Cino's poetry and views were, like Celso's, grounded in a more down-to-earth and realistic awareness of the love experience. Such an analysis separated Cino and his beloved from the standard relationships of *Dolce stil nuovo* poets with their "angelic lady," like Dante's relationship with Beatrice. Cino's Selvaggia, much like Celso's, is a flesh-and-blood woman, not "a thing come upon earth from heaven to show forth a miracle."[17] Although the beloved's beauty may be a reflection of heavenly beauty and an object of contemplation, it is not a heaven-sent wonder. It is, instead, an earthly reflection of heavenly perfection.

The standard elements of *Dolce stil nuovo* love poetry were further developed in the fourteenth century by Petrarch and in the sixteenth by Petrarchan poets and theorists. Among the various aspects of courtly love which Firenzuola has appropriated and echoes in his dialogue between Celso and the ladies are the secret nature of such love, the lover's anguish at the beloved's unawareness of his devotion, his consequent suffering at being unnoticed and having his love unreciprocated, the cryptic words uttered in trying to speak of this secret love, and his simulated attention or affection for another lady who functions as a screen in order to deflect idle gossip from the true beloved. Verdespina, with the innocence and exuberance of youth, admits her confusion and impatience with such games and speaks bluntly to Celso, telling him to be more open and direct in his courtship. However, Selvaggia and the older women are not confused by Celso's words and glances. They share with the reader the awareness of a subtext of sexual innuendo and playful teasing running between Celso and Selvaggia, a subtext meant to attract mutual attention and raise desire.

At an encomiastic level the dialogue is Firenzuola's elegant exercise in singing the praises of Selvaggia Rocchi, the beautiful young woman whom he had taken as his poetical muse and to whom he had addressed several of his poems.[18] The author describes her beauty, presents her lively character, and, through the *persona* of Celso, flirts with her in a manner that would not have been proper for Firenzuola himself, a Vallambrosian monk and abbot. In the elegy "Although my badly written pages" ("Ancorché le mie mal vergate carte"), Firenzuola recalls how he attempted to depict the ideal beauty in his dialogue *On the Beauty of Women* and then explains to Selvaggia, the recipient of the elegy, why in the *Dialogue* he gave her the fictitious name of Amorrorisca—he claims to have seen a beautiful woman descend from heaven, bearing that name engraved in gold letters on her forehead, and to have heard a sweet voice from above declare: "Amorrorisca means a gentle yoke."[19] The elegy, written to a Selvaggia who was now a wife and mother, may be Firenzuola's attempt to redefine the terms of reference and thus redeem Selvaggia's role as his muse.

Intellectual Background to Renaissance Neoplatonism

The intellectual climate of sixteenth-century Italy was dominated to a large extent by Neoplatonic philosophy. In fact, the study of Plato had been gaining importance in Italy since the middle of the fifteenth century, and there had been interest in it as early as the fourteenth century. Francesco Petrarch (1304–1374) and Giovanni Boccaccio (1313–1375), while unable to read Greek themselves—they both sought, unsuccessfully, to learn it—had become patrons of Greek letters and held Greek authors and manuscripts in high esteem. Petrarch, for example, expressed the bittersweet joy of receiving a Greek manuscript of Homer in his letter to Nicholas Sygeros, saying your Homer is dumb to me, or rather I am deaf to him. Nevertheless I rejoice at his mere physical presence; often I clasp him to my bosom and say with a sigh: "O great man, how gladly would I hear you speak!" . . . I have long had a copy of Plato; it came to me from the west, rather remarkably. . . . Now by your bounty the prince of Greek poets joins the prince of philosophers. Who would not rejoice and glory in housing such guests? I have indeed of both of them all that has been translated into Latin from their own tongue. But it is certainly a pleasure, though no advantage, to regard the Greeks in their own dress. Nor have the years robbed me of all hope of making progress in your language.[20]

Boccaccio and Petrarch learned the rudiments of Greek from a Calabrian, Leontius Pilatus, whom they commissioned to translate Homer into Latin.[21] In 1360, Boccaccio established a chair of Greek Studies at Florence for Pilatus. Although not an entirely successful venture, this early commitment to Greek learning was taken up by later humanists who studied both the language and thought of Greek antiquity.

The study of Greek letters in the Italian peninsula was also fostered by a series of unrelated events. In 1439, Pope Eugenius IV convoked an ecumenical council to reunite the divided Greek and Latin churches. The Council of Florence brought together the leaders of the Catholic and Orthodox churches and, as host city, considerable prestige accrued to Florence. The presence of the large Byzantine delegation, which included the Emperor himself, did much to stimulate interest in Greek learning. The Florentine humanists took advantage of this unprecedented opportunity to discuss philosophy with some of the leading fifteenth-century Platonists who were members of the Orthodox delegation. Stimulated by the atmosphere surrounding the Council, Ambrogio Traversari began translating the Greek Fathers into Latin.

Greek learning was further enhanced by the interest and patronage of Pope Nicholas V (1397–1455, elected 1447), a humanist by training and by inclination, whose love of Greek antiquity influenced his approach to contemporary problems. Nicholas wanted to bring together in one place the sum of ancient learning and in the process founded the Vatican Library. In addition to collecting books, he patronized scholars and translators of the Greek classics. He gathered some of the period's leading Graecists around the papal court at Rome, including such illustrious figures as Lorenzo Valla (1407–1457) and the Greeks George of Trebizond (1395–1472/3) and Theodore Gaza (1398–1478). It was as a result of Nicholas's patronage of Greek that the distinguishing characteristic of humanist learning came to be not facility in Latin, but rather a knowledge of Greek.

Another factor that dramatically contributed to an increase in the study of Greek letters was the Fall of Constantinople (1453). In the years preceding the ultimate collapse of the Byzantine Empire, a stream of Greek emigrés had moved to the West, bringing with them their books, their language, and their philosophy. Perhaps the most important was Cardinal Bessarion (c.1395–1472), who originally went to Italy as a member of the Orthodox delegation to the Council of Florence and ultimately remained, joining the Roman curia in 1442. By the 1450s Bessarion was the nucleus of a circle of Greek scholars at Rome, exercising patronage and encouraging philosophical debates.

These Greek emigrés were well acquainted with both Plato and Aristotle. Many had been dramatically influenced by George Gemistos Plethon (d. 1452), who had encouraged the study of Platonic philosophy within Byzantine intellectual circles—although not always espousing an interpretation completely compatible with Orthodox theology. In fact, the Patriarch of Constantinople ordered one of Plethon's books destroyed because of its non-Christian Platonic ideas. Plethon himself had taken part in the Council of Florence and, according to Ficino, may have inspired Cosimo de' Medici to found the Platonic Academy.

The culmination of this intellectual interest can be seen in the work of the great Florentine Neoplatonist, Marsilio Ficino (1433–1499). Ficino became the head of the Platonic Academy (founded in 1462) and the leading proponent of Renaissance Neoplatonism. The Academy, a group of scholars, intellectuals, and artists, met at the Medici villa at Careggi. While not a teaching institution, it nevertheless provided Ficino with an atmosphere conducive to his scholarly pursuits and an intellectual community that helped him develop his ideas.

Ficino became the most important translator and commentator on Greek philosophical texts, especially those of Neoplatonic philosophy. His translations of Platonic sources included the *Corpus Hermeticum* (1463), Plato's dialogues (1468), the works of Porphyry and Proclus (1489), and those of Dionysius the Areopagite and Plotinus (1492). In addition, Ficino wrote a number of works of his own, the most important of which are the *Platonic Theology* (written in 1474 but not in circulation until 1487), *On the Christian Religion* (1477), and the *Commentary on Plato's Symposium* (Latin edition 1484; Italian edition 1544).

In his writings, Ficino sought to reconcile the traditional teachings of

Christianity and Neoplatonism in order to arrive at a hybrid doctrine of Christian Neoplatonism. His ideas were immediately popular and came to dominate Italian intellectual circles. Ficino's use of a Platonic intellectual framework to explain traditional religious doctrines was not an innovation but rather an emulation of the methods of the Fathers of the early Church. Unlike the Fathers, however, who incorporated Platonic philosophy in a selective fashion, Ficino sought to reconcile the totality of Platonic thought with Christianity in much the same way that Thomas Aquinas had reconciled Aristotelian philosophy and Christian theology. In so doing, Ficino became the father of Christian Neoplatonism in its Renaissance manifestation.

Ficino started from the premise that Christian doctrine was true and that this truth could be known as much through the intellectual means provided by Platonic philosophy as through divine revelation. For Ficino the Christian's desire for salvation was basically the same as the philosopher's, pagan and Christian alike, that is, pursuit of the highest good. Thus, in Platonic philosophy, the soul's desire to ascend to truth and goodness became analogous with the Christian's desire for salvation and the vision of God. This desire to ascend was seen as innate in all creation because God's perfection would naturally attract all beings to Him. Thus, all creation emanates from God and desires to return to its origins, that is, to the goodness of God, in which each being will be perfected. In humanity, the higher nature—the soul—yearns to ascend to God. Human beings, however, have a dual nature, and like other animals can be motivated by lower, physical desires. Only through the application of reason and contemplation can a person direct the soul away from the body, toward truth and beauty and, ultimately, to God.

Ideas such as the soul's ascent to God through contemplation of beauty were particularly sympathetic in a milieu that was at once orthodox Christian and obsessed by the pursuit of art and culture. In the sixteenth century, writers adopted the literary genre favored by Plato himself and produced a multitude of dialogues on the theme of "Platonic love." The term was first coined by Ficino to refer to Plato's concept of spiritual love, a passionate friendship modeled upon the relationships between the heroes of Greek mythology. Renaissance dialogues on this topic clearly developed the interrelationship of love and beauty as first expressed by Plato in his *Symposium:* love was perceived as the effect of beauty on the beholder, and physical beauty as the outward manifestation of inner beauty, that is, goodness. Within this conceptual framework, love of beauty equaled love of goodness and thus contemplation upon the beautiful—that is, the good—aided the soul's ascent to God.

This conceptual framework was something of a departure from the more ambivalent and dualist understanding of the physical world prevalent in the Middle Ages. While medieval philosophers and theologians recognized that all material reality was God's good creation, they nevertheless were influenced by dualist thought which established a set of binary oppositions that juxtaposed physical with spiritual, bad with good. Thus, the physical order was viewed with a certain suspicion and was perceived as having the potential to draw humanity away from the higher, rational, spiritual order that led to salvation. For example, Bernard of Clairvaux rejected all forms of beauty, natural or artistic, as having the potential to distract him from spiritual matters. This may be contrasted with Thomas Aquinas's conclusion that "beauty and goodness are inseparable."[22] Thus, while physical beauty was understood as a reflection of God's creative good, it was also viewed as having the potential to draw humanity away from the spiritual and to incite more earthly, possibly sinful, desires.

During the Renaissance, on the other hand, the influence of Neoplatonism evaluated the physical world as unequivocally positive and saw it as a first step toward a greater appreciation of the spiritual realm. The body was not necessarily an impediment to salvation but rather could contribute to it by leading the soul to meditate first on physical, outer beauty, and then on spiritual, inner beauty. Eventually the lover would raise his contemplation to the ultimate beauty which is God.

The proliferation of the Neoplatonic dialogues helped to disseminate and popularize the ideas developed by Ficino in his *Commentary on Plato's Symposium*. Although the Latin version of the *Commentary* had been published in 1484, the Italian translation was not printed until 1544. As a result, the popularization of Ficino's ideas about Platonic love was primarily the result of the work of others, and especially of the authors of dialogues written in Italian. These vernacular works were in the main responsible for transmitting the Neoplatonic philosophy of love to a wider and less-learned audience than that which had frequented the Florentine Academy.

One of the most famous and enduring of these popularizing, Neoplatonic dialogues was *The Book of the Courtier* (completed 1518, printed 1528) by Baldassare Castiglione (1478–1529).[23] *The Courtier* provides a clear example of how such works were frequently written to bring honor upon a specific group, in this case the court of Elisabetta Gonzaga, Duchess of

Urbino, whose members provided the inspiration and the personae for the characters in the dialogue. The discussion recorded in *The Courtier* purports to have been the postprandial entertainment on three successive evenings in 1506. The interlocutors, who include some of the most prestigious and noble figures of the time, are set the task of describing the attributes of the ideal courtier. The participants describe the ideal courtly society and the qualities and skills valued in the ideal courtier, male and female alike. In the course of this discussion, the ideal form of love is also described. Book IV provides an eloquent exposition of Neoplatonic love and the ascent of the soul, enraptured first by earthly beauty and then by abstract, divine beauty. The focus of the discussion in *The Book of the Courtier* is on the ideal, and it acquires a quality of otherworldliness. The tone is overwhelmingly one of high culture seeking to distance itself from the harsh realities of daily life.

Another work, appearing in the same historical context but directed toward a different audience and reflecting a different value system, is the *Galateo* by Giovanni Della Casa (1503–1556).[24] The *Galateo,* although a courtesy book, is infused with the personal values of a social group very different from that of Castiglione. Della Casa was a member of an old Florentine republican family. His book presupposes the man who is active in the world and participating in current affairs. Thus the audience of the *Galateo* is that of a sophisticated and educated urban patriciate, one used to the exercise of political power and self-government. Della Casa's advice, then, was directed at a very different constituency from that of Castiglione. Rather than concentrating on the ideal as a refuge from the harsh realities of life, Della Casa concentrates on those qualities necessary for a man to negotiate the treacherous waters of contemporary political affairs.

Firenzuola's *On the Beauty of Women* fits clearly into this established pattern, yet it is also unique and innovative. While seeking to bring honor to his acquaintances, Firenzuola's context is neither the glittering circle of a court nor a sophisticated urban elite. Rather, his audience and context are at once more bourgeois and more provincial than those of either Castiglione or Della Casa. The interlocutors, neither illustrious nor learned, are the bourgeois inhabitants of Prato, a quiet provincial town near Florence. Thus Firenzuola takes the task of popularizing Neoplatonic thought a step further: he leaves the learned humanist circles of the elite and preaches the doctrines of Neoplatonism in the haunts frequented by his primarily middle-class audience. With works such as Firenzuola's, Neoplatonism was no longer the philosophy of the learned and their wealthy court patrons, but had entered the mainstream and become the ideology of a broad spectrum of Renaissance society.

Firenzuola, Neoplatonism, and Art

The adaptation of Neoplatonic ideas about love by artists and patrons alike established a mutually reinforcing relationship between philosophy and art. Neoplatonism provided the intellectual underpinnings for society's appreciation and cultivation of fine arts, while art provided those beautiful objects so necessary for the soul's contemplation and ascent. In Book V of his *Commentary on Plato's Symposium,* Ficino developed a lengthy discussion of what constituted beauty of the body, linking together spiritual goodness and physical attributes such as the arrangement of limbs, their proportion, shape, and color. He thus set the stage for later treatises, like that of Firenzuola, which sought to link philosophy with more mundane artistic theory.

In *On the Beauty of Women* the influence of Neoplatonic philosophy is clear and pervasive. For example, Firenzuola states that "a beautiful woman is the most beautiful object one can admire, and beauty is the greatest gift God bestowed on His human creatures. And so, through her virtue we direct our souls to contemplation, and through contemplation to the desire for heavenly things" (p. 11, below). No clearer statement of the philosophical underpinnings of Firenzuola's presentation could be provided. By his clear and explicit linking of woman's external beauty with inner goodness and virtue, the Neoplatonic idea of the relationship between macrocosm and microcosm was extended to the nature of women.

Firenzuola also shows clearly the influence of traditional, mathematically based artistic theory. This theory was developed by the Roman writer Vitruvius, in his *Ten Books on Architecture,* and was mediated to Renaissance audiences by writers such as Leon Battista Alberti in his works *On Painting* and *On Sculpture.* Firenzuola provides a lengthy, mathematical discussion on the correct proportion of the limbs of a woman's body in which the influence of Vitruvius is unmistakable, including the notion that the human form, with arms extended, should fit exactly into a square and that each part of the body should be in direct proportion to the others. In this Firenzuola followed Alberti in preferring to use the head as the unit of measure rather than the foot, as Vitruvius had done.[25]

Thus, Firenzuola was aware of his place in a long line of ancient and Renaissance writers on artistic theory. He consciously placed himself in the tradition of the Greek painter Zeuxis, who was said to have painted a composite portrait of perfect beauty. The story of Zeuxis was popular in Antiquity and often repeated in the Renaissance by Alberti and others (see p. 13, below, for Firenzuola's discussion of Zeuxis). By identifying himself within this tradition, Firenzuola was at once acknowledging his debt to his predecessors, both ancient and modern, and investing his own ideas with an equivalent authority.

Ideas about the Nature of Women

In the Renaissance there developed a great debate about the nature of women, the *querelle des femmes*. Central to this debate are questions about human nature that endure until today. Are men and women essentially the same or are they essentially different? Are gender differences biologically determined or socially constructed?

Traditionally, there have been two basic approaches to these questions, represented by the ideas of the two great philosophers of Antiquity: Plato and Aristotle. The Aristotelian interpretation can be summarized as teaching that men and women are essentially different and that women, by their very nature, are subordinate to men. The Platonic school, on the other hand, believed that both possessed essentially the same nature and only their bodies, their outer shells, were different. In its original form, then, the Platonic evaluation was one of gender equality. Over time, however, philosophers did suggest that while women were spiritually and morally equal, they were socially subordinate because of their biological function in procreation.

This development was compatible with traditional Christian teaching about the equality of souls. With the revival of Aristotelian philosophy and its reconciliation with Christian theology by Thomas Aquinas in the thirteenth century, however, the view of the essential inequality of the sexes came to dominate in intellectual circles. The result was the appearance of many treatises using Aristotelian philosophy to justify women's subordinate place in society.[26]

With the fifteenth-century revival of Neoplatonic thought, the notion of the essential equality of men and women came to the fore once again. Renaissance defenders of women, however, could not break completely free from their intellectual roots and continued to be influenced by residual Aristotelianism. Consequently, discussions of women's abilities and equality with men were frequently couched in terms of their innate weaknesses and appropriate social inferiority. This attitude may be seen clearly in Boccaccio's *De claris mulieribus*,[27] which praises women either for their "manly" accomplishments or for their more conventional female virtues.

This attitude is also reflected in the *Libri della famiglia* by the influential Florentine humanist Leon Battista Alberti.[28] Alberti presents a vision of the ideal woman as one who is passive and obedient to her husband. She is also eminently well suited for childbearing and therefore able to provide children for her husband's greater honor. While some participants in the dialogue seek to mitigate misogynistic excesses, the ultimate view of women presented by Alberti is one of passivity and objectification. Thus, even authors who have been characterized as defenders of women continued to measure them against a standard of masculine achievement in the world while concomitantly embracing a double standard of feminine qualities of chastity, humility, and modesty.

Writers who appeared less ambivalent and presented a positive evaluation of women's nature may frequently have been influenced more by pragmatic considerations than by Neoplatonic philosophy. For example, motives of dependency and patronage may underlie Bartolommeo Goggio's fifteenth-century treatise *De laudibus mulierum*. While arguing for women's innate superiority over men, Goggio nevertheless must have composed his work with a conscious awareness of how it would be received by its dedicatee, Eleonora of Aragon, Duchess of Ferrara.[29]

Although Renaissance Neoplatonic philosophers would concede to women an equality of nature, they nevertheless continued to espouse and reinforce the Aristotelian notion of women's social and spiritual inferiority. Women were not understood or evaluated as the appropriate companions described in such treatises exalting Platonic love and friendship as those by Marsilio Ficino and Leone Ebreo.[30] Because Neoplatonic friendships required a reciprocal nobility of spirit that could not exist across the social and intellectual chasms dividing women and men, many Renaissance defenses of women are rightly viewed as ambivalent at best. Constance Jordan has pointed out that "treatises ostensibly *defending* women are sometimes ambiguous because their intention is in fact twofold and to a degree contradictory. They are designed both to praise and to blame women, to allow them a dignified and honored place in society while at the same time demonstrating that this place is beneath that of men."[31]

Against this background, Firenzuola is an anomaly. His evaluation of gender is neither one of female inferiority nor backhanded complementarity. Based on his understanding of the creation story narrated by Aristophanes in Plato's *Symposium,* he clearly asserts the equality of women and men in every aspect of life. The story, one of the most popular in the Renaissance, asserts that men and women were originally united in one being and therefore possess identical natures; yet few writers were sufficiently courageous or imaginative to push this idea to its logical conclusion and to assert unequivocally the equality of men and women. In concluding so, Firenzuola departed significantly from the standard understanding of the *Symposium* and advanced his own unique interpretation of Neoplatonic philosophy. Almost one hundred years later, Cristoforo Bronzini drew upon this same theoretical basis to make this very point, an indication of the continuing strength of Aristotelianism and the depth of the resistance to notions of gender equality among a masculinist intellectual elite.[32]

For Firenzuola and Bronzini, as for Plato earlier, men and women have the same natures and abilities. For both writers, it is social constraints that relegate women to subordinate positions and restrict their opportunities. In this respect, Firenzuola differed from the contemporary understanding of gender in humanist, Neoplatonic, and masculinist circles. Despite his clerical vocation, Firenzuola was a man of the world, one who knew women and liked them. Released from the constraints of princely court society and the philosophical pretentiousness of learned circles, Firenzuola felt free, in the provincial society of Prato, to express his own beliefs and something of the social context and interaction he saw around him.[33] While ideology may have reinforced the subordination of women, it seems clear that in daily life, at least at the more modest levels of society, women interacted more freely and equally with men than the prevalent discourse of misogyny would suggest.[34]

Thus while *On the Beauty of Women* appears at first glance to fit neatly into the genre of defenses of women, it is in fact unique. Firenzuola drew from his ideas their logical conclusion. In the process, he followed the thread of Renaissance Neoplatonism past the constraints of convention and allowed for a new vision of the relationships between men and women, one predicated on notions of equality and respect, to emerge. In doing so, Firenzuola may be justly credited with bringing a feminist[35] sensibility to his discussion and with offering his society an alternative direction in which to develop. As he concludes about the relations of women and men, "we are one and the same thing, one and the same perfection, and . . . you must seek us and love us, and we must seek and love you, and you are nothing without us, and we are nothing without you, our perfection is in you, and yours in us" (p. 21).

Critical Comments on the Dialogue *On the Beauty of Women*

Jakob Burckhardt called Firenzuola's dialogue on feminine beauty "remarkable."[36] According to Burckhardt, Firenzuola subordinated general aesthetic principles to the close scrutiny of particulars, for such "ultimate principles of beauty . . . are a secret even for Firenzuola." Burckhardt then concluded that "no other work can be compared to that of Firenzuola."[37] Luigi Tonelli concurs with Burckhardt and, giving vent to critical hyperbole, calls "the little treatise by the most elegant Florentine abbot . . . the most important work of Renaissance pedagogical literature on feminine beauty, and the most reliable evidence of the new aesthetic sensibility, inspired by both Platonism and Petrarchism."[38]

The Italian critic Natalino Sapegno pointed out that Firenzuola was highly esteemed in his own time. The dialogue *On the Beauty of Women* was "one of the most interesting documents of the aesthetic ideal of the sixteenth century, with its sense of grace, measure, harmony, . . . which animates all the art and poetry of that century and which surfaces also in the typical feminine creations of Ariosto."[39]

Delmo Maestri, Firenzuola's most recent editor, placed the work within the context of mid-sixteenth-century Tuscany and its "tired, provincial" culture. He claimed that the premise of discussing and then visualizing perfect feminine beauty by choosing the best elements of the four women who form a circle around Celso blended wonderfully the high themes of love and beauty with the low counterpoint of a lively, gallant conversation. According to Maestri, aesthetic arguments are dropped gently to the plane of colloquial discourse, and difficulties are simplified. Beauty, for example, is not defined, but illustrated in current vocabulary and with contemporary examples. The result is an open, airy, very human image of the familiar idyll. For Maestri, the image of Celso chatting with his beautiful lady-friends on the hill covered with cypresses and laurel trees in the garden of the former Abbey of Grignano was one of the most unforgettable in Italian Renaissance literature.[40]

Firenzuola's treatise first attracted the attention of English-speaking audiences as a result of Elizabeth Cropper's important analysis of contemporary paintings, especially those by Parmigianino, against the aesthetics presented in the *Delle bellezze delle donne*. Cropper's close reading of Firenzuola's artistic theory is important for understanding sixteenth-century aesthetics and Firenzuola's place in this discourse. She concludes that this work "is probably the most complete exposition of the beauty of the ideal woman among the multitude of sixteenth-century treatments of the theme."[41] Tonia Caterina Riviello claims it "an important historical document, showing the symbiotic relations between the philosophers and the painters of the sixteenth-century Florentine courts."[42] Mary Rogers has examined Firenzuola in the context of similar treatises by Trissino and Luigini. She concludes that Firenzuola's treatise "is the only one of the three . . . which attempts any serious examination of the nature and purpose of beauty in general, and woman's beauty in particular."[43] These comments illustrate clearly the importance of the dialogue *On the Beauty of Women* for the study of sixteenth-century views on beauty, aesthetics, and artistic theory.

Translation Criteria

The present translation has been drawn from the critical edition of the *Opere* of Agnolo Firenzuola edited by Delmo Maestri ([Torino: UTET, 1977], pp. 713–89). It was then carefully read against the *editio princeps* of 1548. We have also consulted the editions by Giuseppe Fatini (*Opere scelte* [Torino: UTET, 1957; 2nd ed. 1966], pp. 467–549); Adriano Seroni (*Opere* [Firenze: Sansoni, 1958; 2nd ed., 1971], pp. 519–96); and the 1802 edition published in Milan by the Società Tipografica dei Classici Italiani (vol. 5, pp. 1–97).

Although Clara Bell's 1892 translation (London: Osgood, McIlvaine) is not generally a work to be trusted, we did consult it, especially when confronted with difficult readings in the original. At such times, when it was not obvious that Bell was mistranslating a passage, we took advantage of her reading. Occasionally Bell's rendering shed light on an otherwise obscure passage. On the whole, however, her translation is charmingly old-fashioned and fuzzy. She paraphrases—and at times even omits—difficult passages; she has a tendency to attenuate or dissimulate the sexual play and innuendos, especially those between Celso and Selvaggia; she occasionally mistranslates words and passages; and she offers no critical apparatus at all. Hers is not a scholarly translation, nor even a trustworthy one.

With no other English translation available, the need for a reliable, scholarly, and annotated English version was pressing. Firenzuola's work is an important contribution to our understanding of sixteenth-century thinking about women, beauty, balance, elegance, and style. It is an important antidote to the excessive attention scholars have paid to works such as Castiglione's *Book of the Courtier* (Venice, 1528). And it is an ideal companion piece to such popular and successful works as Della Casa's book of manners, the *Galateo* (Venice, 1558).

In translating the text we have made one major change: when it could be done easily, long Italianate sentences have been shortened in order to let English sentences flow more smoothly. In the lively sixteenth-century debate on the *questione della lingua* ("the question of language") Firenzuola sided with, and was a strong supporter of, the contemporary Florentine vernacular. As he says in the Proem, "I have . . . sought to imitate everyday speech, and not the language of Petrarch or Boccaccio. . . . I have always relied upon and used those words and that manner of speech that is bartered all day long, spending the money, as Horace says, that is current tender, not worn-out coins or Saint-Johns-asitting" (p. 7). Given Firenzuola's adherence to the modern Tuscan camp and his strong support for refined contemporary speech, it seemed appropriate to adhere to his guidelines and use a form of English that is, as much as possible, accepted "current tender." That is not to say, however, that a certain amount of contemporary Florentine linguistic flavor has not been retained. On the contrary, we have sought to keep the Tuscan idioms and thus bring to the reader's consciousness an awareness that the text represents the conversations of bourgeois young people in mid-sixteenth-century Prato.

We have retained, when possible, variances in form and style present in the original text because they may point to subtle but important differences in connotation. For example, in the second dialogue the principal speaker, Celso, often alternates between the first person singular and plural in expressions such as "I think" and "We will say"—and this may be seen as an indication that some comments could be viewed as Celso's own personal opinions while others are perhaps a reflection of generally accepted concepts of beauty. Similarly, we have retained the differentiation Firenzuola himself made between the formal, latinate style of the Proem, or introductory section, and the more colloquial, fast-paced prose of the dialogue proper.

Firenzuola's technical vocabulary, especially when describing colors or qualities, is at once vague and precise. That is, the terminology appears to be vague and general, but the consistency in usage of these terms suggests that Firenzuola was paying careful attention to their precise meaning. In order to avoid introducing confusion into our translation, we established the following translation scheme for qualities and colors, and adhered to it consistently:

aria	air
grazia	grace
leggiadria	elegance
maestà	majesty
vaghezza	charm
venustà	loveliness
azzurro	azure blue
bianco	white
biondo	blonde
candido	fair
imbalconato or *incarnato* (used synonymously)	flesh-pink
lionato	tawny
negro	black
rosso	red
tané	tan
vermiglio	vermillion

This scheme allowed us to respect Firenzuola's terminology and retain his nuances between similar but different terms. Thus *venustà,* for example, is always "loveliness" and never any of its synonyms.

We have omitted from the English title the name "Celso," which is sometimes included as a subtitle in Italian editions ("Dialogo delle bellezze delle donne intitolato Celso," in the 1977 edition by Delmo Maestri). Our title is drawn from the title page in the 1548 *editio princeps,* on which the subtitle "Celso" does not yet appear. The use or addition of a subtitle drawn from the name of the principal speaker was not uncommon at the time— for example, Benedetto Varchi's *Ercolano,* Pier Francesco Gianbullari's *Gello,* Giambattista Gelli's *Circe.* In the case of Firenzuola's dialogue, however, the subtitle "Celso" was a later addition, and, therefore, we have preferred to adhere to the earliest form.

Our translation is accompanied by various types of notes. Some are explanations for our translation choices; others are elucidations of references made by Firenzuola. The majority, however, are designed for readers not conversant with Italian history, literature, or thought. In providing the notes we tried to find a balance between the needs of the scholar and those of the student. We trust that the expert will not be distracted by the simplicity of the critical apparatus, nor the neophyte overwhelmed by its weight.

Notes

1. Introduction to *L'asino d'oro,* in the *Opere,* ed. Delmo Maestri (Torino: UTET, 1977), 230; see also in the edition by Adriano Seroni (Florence: Sansoni, 1958; 2nd ed. 1971), 198.

2. Aretino's letter is included in Maestri's edition of Firenzuola's works, pp. 634–35. It can be found also in Aretino's *Opere,* ed. Francesco Flora (Milan: Mondadori, 1960), 809–11. The English translation of this letter, by Thomas C. Chubb in *The Letters of Pietro Aretino* (n.p.: Archon Books, 1967), 172–73, is a paraphrase and is not precise. Aretino's mordant pen led him to style himself "the scourge of princes" and allowed him to live comfortably in a *palazzo* in Venice on the "hush money" paid to him by dignitaries in Italy and abroad.

3. "Nelle belle contrade u' Blanda Fonte" ("In the beautiful neighborhoods where the Branda Fountain") and "Dalle belle contrade che di vecchie" ("From the beautiful neighborhoods that [are called] old"); see *Opere,* ed. Maestri, 997–98.

4. Pietro Bembo (1470–1547), who became a cardinal (1539), was an internationally respected poet, writer, and linguistic theorist. His most famous work, *Writings on the Vernacular Language* (*Prose della volgar lingua,* written in 1506–1512, printed in 1525), became the major Renaissance text on Italian language, grammar, and stylistics.

5. In the *Opere,* ed. Maestri, 634. Chubb's translation of Aretino's letter (see n. 2 above) is incorrect at this point, for it says that Firenzuola read the work to Pope Clement. However, this is not what either Aretino or Firenzuola say (see below, p. 4).

6. See Eugenio Ragni's "Nota biografica" in his edition of Firenzuola's *Le novelle* (Milano: Giovanni Salerno, 1971), xxxiv; and Maestri, "Introduzione" to Firenzuola's *Opere,* 13–15.

7. See below, p. 7.

8. Michele Maylander points out the *Accademia dell'Addiaccio* ("Academy of the Sheep-pen") is not well known, even though it was the first to be founded in Prato. The Academy, founded by Firenzuola and his friend Niccolò Martelli, met in the Badia della Sacca and in the villa of the Segni. Members assumed names reminiscent of those of classical Greek shepherds and, in their compositions, sang the praises of rustic life. Because of this, the *Addiaccio* may be seen as a precursor of seventeenth-century Arcadian academies. See Maylander's entry in his *Storia delle Accademie d'Italia,* vol. 1 (Bologna, 1926–1930; rpt. Forni, [1970]), 58–59.

9. Cited in G. Fatini, "Nel IV centenario della morte di Agnolo Firenzuola," *La Rinascita* 6 (1943): 473; also in E. Ragni's edition of *Le novelle,* xxxiv.

10. See his *De imitatione,* 1512, and his *Prose della volgar lingua,* 1525.

11. For Castiglione's views, see his clearly presented argument in the dedicatory letter to *The Book of the Courtier,* trans. Singleton, 3–5.

12. "illustre, cardinale, aulicum esse et curiale," *De vulgari eloquentia,* ed. A. Meozzi (Milano: Carlo Signorelli, 1968), lib. I cap. xix, p. 66. The treatise was written between 1301 and 1321.

13. The letter is dated in Rome, 7 February 1525. Tolomei (1492–1555), a Sienese scholar and nobleman, was also residing in Rome and working in the papal curia.

14. Agnolo Firenzuola, "Epistola in lode delle donne," in *Opere,* ed. Maestri, 217.

15. As reported by Maestri, in Firenzuola's *Opere,* 723 n. 5. See also Giuseppe Fatini, *Agnolo Firenzuola e la borghesia letterata del Rinascimento* (Cortona: Prem. Tipografia Sociale, 1907), 21–22.

16. Cino da Pistoia (c. 1270–c. 1336), the last of the major *dolcestilnovisti,* was a personal friend of both Dante and Petrarch, thus bridging the gap between the late medieval and the early Renaissance poetic schools. Both Dante and Petrarch addressed sonnets to him.

17. The phrase is from Dante's sonnet "Tanto gentile e tanto onesta pare," vv. 7–8. George Kay trans., *The Penguin Book of Italian Verse* (Harmondsworth: Penguin Books, 1958, 1965), 80.

18. These comprise a sonnet ("Spirto gentil, ch'alla beltà terrena"), two elegies ("Ancorché le mie mal vergate carte" and "Come avran fine i cominciati affanni"), as well as a "Selva d'Amore," an octave sequence in praise of Selvaggia. There are also a number of poems not explicitly addressed to Selvaggia which are, in fact, inspired by her and even mention her by name in their verses.

19. We have not been able to corroborate such a meaning. This may be another example of Firenzuola's tendency to create his own etymologies.

20. *Epistolae familiares* XVIII, 2 (10 January 1354) in David Thompson, trans., *Petrarch. An Anthology* (New York: Harper and Row, 1971), 132–33. See also Petrarch's letter to Homer, *Epistolae familiares* XXIV, 12, ibid. 131–84.

21. Pilatus's connection with Petrarch and Boccaccio has been examined in depth in Agostino Pertusi, *Leonzio Pilato fra Petrarca e Boccaccio: le sue versioni omeriche negli autografi di Venezia e la cultura greca del primo Umanesimo* (Venice-Rome: Istituto per la Collaborazione culturale, 1964); see, esp. ch. 1, pp. 1–42.

22. Edgar De Bruyne, *The Esthetics of the Middle Ages,* trans. Eileen B. Hennessy (New York: Frederick Ungar, 1969), 169. See also Thomas Aquinas, *Summa theologica,* I.v.4.

23. Baldassare Castiglione, *The Book of the Courtier,* trans. Charles S. Singleton (Garden City, NY: Doubleday, 1959).

24. Giovanni Della Casa, *Galateo,* trans. Konrad Eisenbichler and Kenneth R. Bartlett (Ottawa: Dovehouse, 1986; 2nd ed. 1990).

25. Leon Battista Alberti, *On Painting and On Sculpture,* ed. and trans. Cecil Grayson (London: Phaidon, 1972), 75; Vitruvius, *The Ten Books on Architecture,* trans. Morris H. Morgan (New York: Dover, 1914; rpt. 1960), I.2, 72.

26. See Ian Maclean, *The Renaissance Notion of Woman. A Study in the Fortunes of Scholasticism and Medical Science in European Intellectual Life* (Cambridge: Cambridge University Press, 1980) for an overview of the influence of Aquinas's appropriation of Aristotelianism on subsequent thinking about the nature of men and women.

27. Giovanni Boccaccio, *Concerning Famous Women*, trans. Guido A. Guarino (New Brunswick, NJ: Rutgers University Press, 1963).

28. Leon Battista Alberti, *The Family in Renaissance Florence*, trans. Renée Neu Watkins (Columbia: University of South Carolina Press, 1969).

29. This treatise is discussed by Werner L. Gundersheimer, who takes it at face value as a feminist reflection on the natures of men and women. See "Bartolommeo Goggio: A Feminist in Renaissance Ferrara," *Renaissance Quarterly* 33:2 (1980): 175–200. The same point can be made to explain the more ambiguous "defense" of women presented in Book III of Castiglione's *Book of the Courtier*, written under the patronage of Elisabetta Gonzaga, Duchess of Urbino.

30. Marsilio Ficino, *Commentary on Plato's Symposium on Love*, trans. Sears Jayne, 2nd rev. ed. (Dallas, TX: Spring Publications, 1985); Leone Ebreo, *The Philosophy of Love*, trans. F. Friedeberg-Seeley and Jean H. Barnes (London: Soncino Press, 1937).

31. Constance Jordan, *Renaissance Feminism. Literary Texts and Political Models* (Ithaca, NY: Cornell University Press, 1990), 18–19.

32. Jordan, *Renaissance Feminism*, 266–68.

33. Jacqueline Murray, "Agnolo Firenzuola on Female Sexuality and Women's Equality," *Sixteenth Century Journal* 22:2 (1991): 199–213.

34. See, for example, the discussion by Elaine G. Rosenthal, "The Position of Women in Renaissance Florence: Neither Autonomy nor Subjection," in *Florence and Italy. Renaissance Studies in Honour of Nicolai Rubinstein*, eds. Peter Denley and Caroline Elam, Westfield Publications in Medieval Studies, 2 (London: Westfield College, 1988), 369–81 and Lauro Martines, "A Way of Looking at Women in Renaissance Florence," *Journal of Medieval and Renaissance Studies* 4 (1974): 15–28.

35. Feminist is here used in its broad sense, referring to those who espouse the notion of the equality of men and women and who seek to rectify women's historically disadvantaged position. Firenzuola surely warrants being described in this manner, given his belief that women and men were essentially the same and that women's apparent inferiority was only socially constructed.

36. Jakob Burckhardt, *The Civilization of the Renaissance in Italy*, trans. S. G. C. Middlemore (New York: Mentor, 1960), 250.

37. *Ibid*, 252.

38. "Il trattatello dell'elegantissimo abate fiorentino rimane, dunque, la più importante opera della precettistica rinascimentale, riguardante la bellezza muliebre; e anche la più sicura testimonianza del nuovo tipo estetico, ispirato bensì dal platonismo e dal petrarchismo." Luigi Tonelli, *L'amore nella poesia e nei trattati del rinascimento* (Florence: G. C. Sansoni, 1933), 298.

39. Natalino Sapegno, *Disegno storico della letteratura italiana* (Firenze: La Nuova Italia, 1949; 1973), 272.

40. Maestri, "Introduzione," in *Opere*, 18–19.

41. Elizabeth Cropper, "On Beautiful Women, Parmigianino, Petrarchismo, and the Vernacular Style," *The Art Bulletin,* 58 (1976): 374.

42. Tonia Caterina Riviello, *Agnolo Firenzuola: The Androgynous Vision,* Biblioteca di Cultura, 325 (Roma: Bulzoni, 1986), 68.

43. Mary Rogers, "The Decorum of Women's Beauty: Trissino, Firenzuola, Luigini and the Representation of Women in Sixteenth-Century Painting," *Renaissance Studies* 2:1 (1988): 66.

Bibliography

WORKS BY FIRENZUOLA

FIRST EDITIONS (IN CHRONOLOGICAL ORDER)

Discacciamento de le nuove lettere inutilmente aggiunte ne la lingua toscana [*The Expulsion of the New Letters Unnecessarily Added to the Tuscan Language*]. Rome: Presso Ludovico Vicentino et Lauditio Perugino, 1524.

Canzone in lode della salciccia [*Song in Praise of the Sausage*] in [Francesco Beccuti] *Commento del Grappa sopra la canzone del Firenzuola in lode alla salsiccia*. Venice: [Iacopo Ruffinelli], 1545; rpt. Bologna: Romagnoli, 1881.

Prose. Edited by Lorenzo Scala and Ludovico Domenichi, 2 vols. Florence: Appresso Bernardo di Giunta, 1548.

Vol. 1: *La prima veste dei discorsi degli animali* [*The First Version of the Animals' Discourses*], ff. 4r–55v; *Dialogo . . . delle bellezze delle donne* [*Dialogue on the Beauty of Women*], ff. 56r–108v; *Elegia a Selvaggia* [*Elegy to Selvaggia*], ff. 109r–112r.

Vol. 2: *Epistola in lode delle donne* [*Letter in Praise of Women*], ff. 6r–11r; *I Ragionamenti d'amore* [*The Discourses on Love*], ff. 11v–72v; *Novelle pratesi* [*Prato Tales*], ff. 73r–84v; and *Discacciamento delle nuove lettere . . .* [*Expulsion of the New Letters . . .*], ff. 85r–96r.

Le rime [*The Poems*]. Florence: Appresso Bernardo Giunti, 1549.

La Trinuzia [*The Triple Marriage*]. Florence: Appresso Bernardo Giunti, 1549.

I Lucidi [*The Lucidi*]. Florence: Appresso Bernardo Giunti, 1549.

Apuleio. Dell'Asino d'oro [*Apuleius. The Golden Ass*]. Venice: Appresso Gabriel Giolito de' Ferrari, 1550.

MODERN ITALIAN EDITIONS (IN CHRONOLOGICAL ORDER)

Opere scelte. Edited by Giuseppe Fatini. Torino: UTET, 1957; 2nd ed., 1966. Pp. 467–549.

Opere. Edited by Adriano Seroni. Firenze: Sansoni, 1958; 2nd ed., 1971. Pp. xlvii, 519–96.

Opere. Edited by Delmo Maestri. Torino: UTET, 1977. Pp. 713–89.

TRANSLATIONS (IN CHRONOLOGICAL ORDER)

Plaisant et facétieux discours des animaux, avec une histoire non moins véritable que plaisante, advenue puis n'a guières en la ville de Florence. Translated by Gabriel Cottier. Lyon, 1556.

Deux livres de filosofie fabuleuse. Le premier prins des discours de M. Ange Firenzuola Florentin. Par lequel subs le sens allegoric de plusieurs belles fables, est montrée l'envye, malice & trahison d'aucuns courtisans. Le second, extraict des Traictez de Sandebar Indien Philosophe moral, traictant soubs pareilles allegories de l'Amitié & choses semblables. Translated by Pierre de la Rivey. Paris: Abel l'Angelier, 1577; rpt. Lyon: B. Rigaud, 1579.

Discours de la beauté des dames, prins de l'italien du seigneur Ange Firenzuola. Translated by Jean Pallet. Paris: Abel l'Angelier, 1578.

Nouvelles de Agnolo Firenzuola. Translated by Alcide Bonneau. Paris: Isidore Liseux, 1881; rpt. Paris: Bibliothèque des Curieux, 1913.

Of the Beauty of Women. Dialogue by Messer Agnolo Firenzuola Florentine. Translated by Clara Bell, introduction by Theodore Child. London: James R. Osgood, McIlvaine, 1892.

Gespräche über die Schönheit der Frauen. Translated by Paul Seliger. Leipzig: J. Hegner, 1903.

Novellen und Gespräche. Translated by Albert Wesselski. Munich: G. Müller, 1910.

Tales of Firenzuola. Translated anonymously. Paris: Isidore Liseux, 1889; rpt. New York: Firenzuola Society, 1929; New York: Valhalla Books, 1964; New York: Italica Press, 1987.

The Bawdy Tales of Firenzuola. Translated by Jules Griffon. Covina, CA: Collectors Publications, 1967.

RECENT CRITICAL WORKS

The following list of critical works in English and in Italian has been drawn from our own readings and from a thorough search of the two major bibliographies in the field: the *Bibliographie Internationale d'Humanisme et Renaissance,* 1–21 (1965–1986) and the *MLA Bibliography,* 1969–1990. Undeservedly, little critical attention has been paid to Firenzuola. The bibliography we provide includes all that has been written on him in the last quarter-century. We have found no recent critical works on Firenzuola in a language other than Italian or English.

ENGLISH-LANGUAGE CRITICISM

Cropper, Elizabeth. "On Beautiful Women, Parmigianino, *Petrarchismo* and the Vernacular Style." *Art Bulletin* 58 (1976): 374–94.

Fahy, Connor. "Three Early Renaissance Treatises on Women." *Italian Studies* 11 (1956): 30–55. Contains an appendix listing forty-one "Treatises on the equality or superiority of women written or published in Italy during the fifteenth and sixteenth centuries," pp. 47–54.

Huffman, Claire L. and Clifford Chambers Huffman. "Firenzuola, Surrey and Watson Once More." *Revue des langues vivantes* 42 (1976): 403–14.

Murray, Jacqueline. "Agnolo Firenzuola on Female Sexuality and Women's Equality." *Sixteenth Century Journal* 22:2 (1991): 199–213.

Riviello, Tonia Caterina. *Agnolo Firenzuola: The Androgynous Vision*. Biblioteca di Cultura, 325. Roma: Bulzoni, 1986.

Rogers, Mary. "The Decorum of Women's Beauty: Trissino, Firenzuola, Luigini and the Representation of Women in Sixteenth-Century Painting." *Renaissance Studies* 2:1 (1988): 47–88.

Thompson, Patricia. "Firenzuola, Surrey and Watson." *Renaissance News* 18 (1965): 295–98.

ITALIAN-LANGUAGE CRITICISM

Two published bibliographies on Firenzuola give a listing of critical works published up to the middle of this century.

Oliveri, Mario. "Bibliografia essenziale ragionata del Firenzuola." *Rivista di sintesi letteraria* 1:3 (1934): 390–400.

Seroni, Adriano. *Bibliografia essenziale delle opere di Agnolo Firenzuola*. Amor di libro 25. Florence: Sansoni Antiquariato, 1957.

For subsequent works see the bibliographies included in the *Opere* edited by Ragni (pp. xxxvii–xxxviii), Seroni (pp. xlvi–xlvii), and Maestri (pp. 30–35).

The following works either have appeared since Maestri's bibliography (1977) or are not included in it.

Cerreta, Florindo. "Una canzone del Firenzuola e una vecchia teoria sulla paternità della commedia degl'*Ingannati*." *La Bibliofilia* 73:2 (1971): 151–63.

Cocco, Mia. "*De la beauté* di Gabriel de Minuit: imitazione cinquecentesca del *Dialogo delle bellezze delle donne* di Agnolo Firenzuola." *Rivista di studi italiani* 2:2 (1984): 10–26.

Maniscalco, Silvana. "Criteri e sensibilità di Agnolo Firenzuola, traduttore di Apuleio." *Rassegna di letteratura italiana* 82 (1978): 88–109.

Romei, Danilo. *La "maniera" romana di Agnolo Firenzuola (dicembre 1524–maggio 1525)*. Florence: Centro 2P, 1983.

———. "Lucrezia, il Firenzuola, la poesia: 1522." *Filologia e critica* 11 (1986): 66–74.

Scarci, Amalia Manuela. "Imitazione e sovvertimento dei modelli nei *Ragionamenti* di Agnolo Firenzuola." Ph.D. dissertation, University of Toronto, 1989.

Seroni, Adriano. "Poesia ideologica nel canzoniere di Agnolo Firenzuola." *Approdo letterario* n.s. 23:79–80 (1977): 99–103.

FURTHER READING

WOMEN IN THE RENAISSANCE

Alberti, Leon Battista. *The Family in Renaissance Florence*. Translated by Renée Neu
    Watkins. Columbia: University of South Carolina Press, 1969.
Allen, Prudence. *The Concept of Woman. The Aristotelian Revolution 750 BC–AD 1250*.
    Montreal: Eden Press, 1985.
Bassanese, Fiona. "What's in a Name? Self-Naming and Renaissance Women Po-
    ets." *Annali d'Italianistica* 7 (1989): 104–15.
Beyond Their Sex. Learned Women of the European Past. Edited by Patricia H.
    Labalme. New York: New York University Press, 1980.
Boccaccio, Giovanni. *Concerning Famous Women*. Translated by Guido A. Guarino.
    New Brunswick, NJ: Rutgers University Press, 1963.
Gottlieb, Beatrice. "The Problem of Feminism in the Fifteenth Century." In *Women
    of the Medieval World*. Edited by Julius Kirshner and Suzanne F. Wemple.
    Oxford: Blackwell, 1985. Pp. 337–64.
Gundersheimer, Werner L. "Bartolommeo Goggio: A Feminist in Renaissance
    Ferrara." *Renaissance Quarterly* 33:2 (1980): 175–200.
*Her Immaculate Hand. Selected Works by and about the Women Humanists of Quattro-
    cento Italy*. Edited and translated by Margaret L. King and Albert Rabil, Jr. Me-
    dieval and Renaissance Texts and Studies, 20. Binghamton, NY: CEMERS,
    1983.
Jordan, Constance. "Boccaccio's In-Famous Women: Gender and Civic Virtue in
    the *De mulieribus claris*." In *Ambiguous Realities. Women in the Middle Ages and
    Renaissance*. Edited by Carole Levin and Jeanie Watson. Detroit, MI: Wayne
    State University Press, 1987. Pp. 25–47.
———. *Renaissance Feminism. Literary Texts and Political Models*. Ithaca, NY: Cor-
    nell University Press, 1990.
Kaufman, Michael W. "Spare Ribs: The Conception of Woman in the Middle Ages
    and the Renaissance." *Soundings* 56 (1973): 139–63.
Kelly, Joan. "Early Feminist Theory and the *Querelle des Femmes*, 1400–1789." In
    Women, History, and Theory. Chicago: University of Chicago Press, 1984.
    Pp. 65–109.
———. "Did Women have a Renaissance?" In *Women, History, and Theory*. Chi-
    cago: University of Chicago Press, 1984. Pp. 19–50.
Kelso, Ruth. *Doctrine for the Lady in the Renaissance*. Urbana: University of Illinois
    Press, 1956.
King, Margaret L. "Caldiera and the Barbaros on Marriage and the Family: Hu-
    manist Reflections of Venetian Realities." *Journal of Medieval and Renaissance
    Studies* 6:1 (1976): 19–50.
———. *Women of the Renaissance*. Women in Culture and Society. Chicago: Univer-
    sity of Chicago Press, 1991.
Labalme, Patricia H. "Venetian Women on Women: Three Early Modern Femi-
    nists." *Archivio Veneto* 117 (1981): 81–109.

Maclean, Ian. *The Renaissance Notion of Woman. A Study in the Fortunes of Scholasticism and Medical Science in European Intellectual Life.* Cambridge: Cambridge University Press, 1980.

Martines, Lauro. "A Way of Looking at Women in Renaissance Florence." *Journal of Medieval and Renaissance Studies* 4 (1974): 15–28.

Price, Paola Malpezzi. "A Woman's Discourse in the Italian Renaissance: Moderata Fonte's *Il merito delle donne*." *Annali d'Italianistica* 7 (1989): 165–81.

Rosenthal, Elaine G. "The Position of Women in Renaissance Florence: Neither Autonomy nor Subjection." In *Florence and Italy. Renaissance Studies in Honour of Nicolai Rubenstein.* Edited by Peter Denley and Caroline Elam. Westfield Publications in Medieval Studies, 2. London: Westfield College, 1988. Pp. 369–81.

Schiesari, Juliana. "In Praise of Virtuous Women? For a Genealogy of Gender Morals in Renaissance Italy." *Quaderni d'Italianistica* 7 (1989): 66–87.

Shemek, Deanna. "That Elusive Object of Desire: Angelica in the *Orlando furioso*." *Annali d'Italianistica* 7 (1989): 116–41.

PHILOSOPHY AND RENAISSANCE NEOPLATONISM

Castiglione, Baldassar. *The Book of the Courtier.* Translated by Charles S. Singleton. Garden City, NY: Doubleday, 1959. There are many other translations available.

Della Casa, Giovanni. *Galateo.* Translated by Konrad Eisenbichler and Kenneth R. Bartlett. Ottawa: Dovehouse, 1986; 2nd ed. 1990.

Ebreo, Leone. *The Philosophy of Love.* Translated by F. Friedeberg-Seeley and Jean H. Barnes. London: Soncino Press, 1937.

Ficino, Marsilio. *Commentary on Plato's Symposium on Love.* Translated by Sears Jayne. Dallas, TX: Spring Publications, 1985.

Kristeller, Paul Oskar. *The Philosophy of Marsilio Ficino.* Translated by Virginia Conant. Gloucester, MA: Peter Smith, 1943; rpt. 1964.

Martines, Lauro. *The Social World of the Florentine Humanists.* Princeton: Princeton University Press, 1963.

Mirandola, Giovanni Pico della. *Oration on the Dignity of Man.* Translated by A. Robert Caponigri. Chicago: Henry Regnery, 1956. There are many other translations available.

Nelson, John Charles. *Renaissance Theory of Love. The Context of Giordano Bruno's Erotici furori.* New York: Columbia University Press, 1958; rpt. 1963.

Plato. *The Symposium.* Translated by Walter Hamilton. Harmondsworth: Penguin Books, 1951; rpt., 1986. There are many other translations available.

Robb, Nesca A. *Neoplatonism of the Italian Renaissance.* London: George Allen and Unwin, 1935; rpt., 1968.

Trinkaus, Charles. *In Our Image and Likeness: Humanity and Divinity in Italian Humanist Thought.* 2 vols. London: Constable, 1970.

On the Beauty
of Women

Proem

Firenzuola, the Florentine,
to the Noble and Fair Ladies of Prato
Greetings.

Having often been asked by those people who have, at all times, the right to command me, that I publish a little dialogue dealing with the perfect beauty of a woman, a work which I composed some time ago at the request of one most dear to me, I believe I can, without too much difficulty, be excused for having been too hesitant or slow in pleasing them. A good number of those people who have asked me know very well how blameworthy and even detrimental it is not to lock up our young and tender little girls in the innermost rooms of our houses, at least until such a time when, letting them go forth, they may, like true offspring of an eagle, withstand the brightness of the sun, and until such a time when that natural affection which every man bears for his own begins to wane and he can see them as something foreign to himself and notice and examine their shortcomings not as a forgiving father but as a strict critic.

I was also diverted from such a purpose by the rumor that some of our local wits, so refined that most of the time they turn into vapor, wanted to discover the names of this or that lady that I have carefully kept hidden. And they were already accosting some ladies and saying: "Don't you know? So-and-so said you use makeup, and he called you Lady Simpleton and Lady Tavern."[1]

And there are some who were not ashamed to claim that one of the beautiful young ladies of Prato, modest and kind, truly a precious flower, is the lady in black satin,[2] thus departing as far from the truth as they were drawing close to the precipice of their own iniquities.

My intention, dear ladies of Prato, was not to point out this or that lady, but rather, thinking that the nature of a dialogue and its embellishments required such little flowers which, like examples, can place the object under discussion in front of the readers, as we are accustomed to do in daily conversation, I made up the name now of one lady, now of another, as the subject of my discourse required, without thinking any more of Mona[3] Pasquina than of Mona Salvestra.[4] Therefore, my beautiful ladies, when these malicious men, who are both your enemies and mine, say that I have spoken badly of you, answer them boldly with what I say all day long, that whoever is apt to give the least offense to the least of our ladies, in thought, word, or deed, is not a man but an animal without reason, a brute. And when such a man speaks badly to you about this or that person, reply, if not in words at least in your mind, that he is not behaving like a true gentleman, for one who speaks badly of someone in his absence, yet smiles to his face, deceives only himself. And do not say anything more, for this answer, being true, will pierce him right through. And so when they say: "This one is so-and-so. That one is so-and-so," I tell you again that they are far from the truth, for the names and surnames I have used were chosen by chance, especially those I used as examples of ugly women.

It is true that some of the names that are there as examples of beauty, as well as those of the four women who converse with Celso, dwell in my imagination and I know them in my thoughts. If someone were to unravel their fictitious names very carefully, he would find their real names covered with a thin veil. And thus this was one of the main reasons why I wanted to let these dialogues grow old in the dust.

Besides which, some people were saying that there were some women who were indignant that I would talk about them, good or bad. Others were unhappy that I should have held them of so little account that I had not given them a place among the four, and thought themselves worthy of it, as indeed they were—as if one could grant such worth to these worthless, unpolished pages of mine, more apt to detract than to heap praise on their good reputation. To these ladies—seeing I am obliged to publish this little work of mine—I will say that the former are wrong since, although my style is low, my eloquence little, the power of my wit feeble, elegance nonexistent, they should at least have accepted my good intentions. That is not to say, however, that my works are not such that some great and illustrious ladies and intelligent gentlewomen in this our Italy did not eagerly read them, appreciate them, and hold their author dear. And I do want and can take pride in this, that the expert ear of Pope Clement VII,[5] whose praise no gifted pen could ever fully sing, in the presence of the best minds of Italy, spent several hours in public paying careful attention to the sound of his own voice as he read the *Expulsion*[6] and the First Day of those *Discourses* I have already dedicated to the most illustrious lady Caterina

Cibo, the most worthy duchess of Camerino.[7] And he did this not without expressing his pleasure or his praises of me. Even if this were not true (though it is very true, and I call on the great Bishop Giovio as a witness),[8] does not Cicero,[9] who was the true measure of Latin prose, write to Lucius Lucceius[10] these very words: "I burn with an incredible desire to be rendered famous by your writings."[11] If, then, the prince of Latin writers shows that he himself holds so dear, burns, even, with the great desire to be rendered famous by the writings of one so inferior to him, so much so that he begs him with such directness to write about him, why are you annoyed if I should mention you or if I should write about you in this little dialogue of mine? For, although I am not Lucius Lucceius (which perhaps I might be), you are neither Helens nor Venuses.[12] I am not speaking about all of you, but only of those women who, if they have not gone deaf in the last few days, I know very well can hear me.[13]

But it may very well be that some of these ladies refuse such praise out of propriety, I mean, humility, that is, because they do not find anything within themselves that would make them worthy of this honor. If this be the case, I readily forgive these ladies; in fact I consider them excused. Turning to the other ladies, who have such a high opinion of this unhappy little booklet of mine that they threaten me with unremitting hatred because I have not included them in it, I tell them, as my true and righteous excuse, that my fear of the former kept me from including the latter, thinking they too would think ill of it, as the former had done. Nonetheless, these ladies who have such a high opinion of my works, I thank them, and whether they bear me a grudge or not, I am nevertheless indebted to them, and one day perhaps I will prove it to them in greater detail.

And another thing that matters not a little has been whispered in my ears, that she who is queen and mistress of my heart, born to be the mainstay of my old age, chosen to be the repose for my weariness, complains that she does not see herself in this work. In the first place, this is no small fault, for I am unaware that any lady knows she is the one for whom I yearn. This is because I have not yet had an occasion to tell her so, nor have I been able to let her know by my actions. Still, if someone has spoken to her on my behalf without my permission, let that person carry this other message to her with my permission, that she should look very carefully at the work, for she is there as one of the four ladies, and that she examine it closely to find herself in it. And if, after all this, she still thinks she is not in it as she would wish, and that she does not recognize herself by any of the clues I have hidden in it, as much as I could, so as not to give people something to talk about, then tell her to look into my heart, through and through, and, if she does not find herself there, then let her speak ill of me. And tell her this should be enough for her and she should not complain about it, but, for the love of God, she should not tell anybody, for this would ruin me.

There are also some busybodies, one of them being the daughter of Mona Biurra dalla Imagine,[14] who say that, because I am ugly, my other half cannot be anything else but as ugly as I am, and as revolting.[15] I must answer these women with some little excuse for myself so as not to be thrown out completely. My ladies, when I was born I was not as old as I am now, nor as hairy, nor as ugly. But the Fates ruined me along the way,[16] and since I have been around a lot and have been out under the sun a lot, I have become as rough and as uncouth as I am, and for this reason I appear to be this dark. But under my doublet I am not as dark as above it, especially on Sunday mornings when I put on a clean shirt. Also, as my mother used to tell me, my wet nurse pulled my nose a little too much.[17] When my beloved and I were parted, we were both equally beautiful; but then, I was marred by a hard life, and she has been well-kept by an easy life.

There are also some who say that, in composing this work, I will lose more than I will gain. They say that, except for the four ladies (actually the three ladies, since one of them has taken offense at having been included and has told me, in person, she neither praises nor thanks me for it), all other ladies have cast me out like a branded heretic.[18] What does it matter? If I were to die at their hands, at least I would not die at the hands of the Turks or the Moors[19] but would die happy, as long as I had not given them just cause, as in truth, till now, I have not. And every time these worthy ladies think of me and remember me, whether kindly or unkindly, I treasure it nonetheless.

I have also heard a woman, who thinks herself wise—and, indeed, she is so—say that I am Celso and, because I lack good neighbors, I have been forced to sing my own praises.[20] But if this lady, or another lady who said this to her and thus the two of them laughed together about me, had done a little more reading, she would have come to appreciate the customary form of dialogues[21] and would not have made such a superficial comment. Still, even if this were not the case and I had intended to present myself as Celso, what praises have I thus bestowed on myself? I have said he is a learned man with an easy-going disposition.[22] If I had not studied and, as a consequence, gained a little learning, it would have been difficult for me to bring this dialogue to its present form. And whether I am learned or not, from now on I want no other proof of it than this little work of mine. If I were not an easygoing fellow, eager to please my friends' wishes, I would not be in this predicament. If I have imagined that Celso has set his love high, pure, holy, on the foundations of virtue, in this, I confess, I do wish to picture myself, and I have described what is true. Nor do I wish to offer any other proof of this than the innocence and purity of my conscience. And if anyone is aware of the least little fault in me, I freely grant him license to disclose it and to prove me a liar. Now you know what to make of these ladies!

There are also some who say that a man of my age or in my profession[23] should not write such works, but rather serious, respectable ones. I will not reply to such people because I have always considered wicked hypocrites, malicious and ignorant people (and those who have said this about me are like that) to be of little or no account, and now I will bother even less with them. And I am sorry that Boccaccio, that worthy man, should have deigned to answer them, for he showed them too much consideration.[24]

There is something else one should not forget to keep in mind, and this is that in everything I have ever written I have not been in the habit of being too careful, as I have not been now, to abide by all the small details of the rules of Tuscan grammar. I have, instead, sought to imitate everyday speech and not the language of Petrarch or Boccaccio.[25] Bearing in mind the words of Favorino,[26] I have always relied upon and used those words and that manner of speech that is bartered all day long, spending the money, as Horace says,[27] that is current tender, not worn-out coins or Saint-Johns-asitting.[28] For this reason, I am sure a good number of those who write professionally will sound the alarm at the many things they will find in my work not in accordance with their rules. But let them do what they want. I have done what I have done because I have wanted to do it like this. If I deserve to be reprimanded for this, let them reprimand me; I will be patient. If they want me to be ashamed, here I am, all red in the face. Nonetheless, so as not to be considered spineless, as soon as I publish my translation of Horace's *Poetics* next summer (it is more like an expanded paraphrase),[29] I will respond with a few words correcting these people.

In the meantime, keep me in your good graces, both for this *Dialogue* and for that little book where foxes and crows speak out, which, as you know, I sent a short while ago to my friends for their comments.[30] Now you see what a predicament I am in, in what a debate I find myself, all because I have gathered together other people's conversations. Nonetheless, I will be so resolute and so strong that I will overcome all these difficulties, like a new Hercules overcoming all these monsters.[31] The respectable wishes of those dear to me will have more effect than any evil tongue or unreasonable obstruction.

I have rewritten them, therefore, with my own hand, and I am determined to let them see the light of day. I have already notified both my friends and my enemies, to whom I will recall that ancient proverb, that only a dead lion will let his beard be cut off.[32]

Dated in Prato, this 18th day of January 1541, under the reign of the Most Illustrious and Excellent Lord Cosimo, most worthy Duke of Florence.

First Dialogue

Celso Selvaggio is a very good friend of mine. I can count on him so much, I often say he is another me. So, if I now publish these dialogues of his, which he once forbade me to do, he will be patient with me, because the love he bears for me forces him to do as I like and, what is more, because I am compelled to do this by someone who can compel him as well. He is also a very learned man, with good judgment, quite easygoing, and very eager to satisfy his friends' wishes. For all these reasons, certain that he will not complain, I have made these dialogues public, as you see.

Last summer, then, he found himself in the garden of the Abbey of Grignano,[1] then rented by Vannozzo Rocchi,[2] where many young ladies, distinguished for their beauty, nobility, and for many other worthy virtues, had gone for a stroll, among whom were Mona Lampiada, Mona Amorrorisca, Selvaggia, and Verdespina. Having withdrawn to the top of a small hill which is in the middle of the garden, all covered with cypress and laurel trees, they were talking about Mona Amelia dalla Torre Nuova, who was still strolling in the garden, and some of them were of the opinion that she was very beautiful and some that she was not at all beautiful. When Celso and some other young men from Prato, who were related to the women mentioned above, came up that same hill, the ladies, caught by surprise, all fell quiet. However, when Celso begged the ladies' pardon for having surprised them, they kindly replied that they welcomed their arrival and invited the young men to sit on a bench that was in front of them, but still they kept quiet. Because of this, Celso once again said:

—Fair ladies, either you carry on with your conversation or bid us leave to go; for we do not wish to play foul with your ball game, but rather to give the ball a kick, should it bounce our way.[3]

Then Mona Lampiada said:

—Messer Celso,[4] ours was women's conversation, and so we did not think it appropriate to continue it in your presence. This lady was saying Amelia is not beautiful, and I was saying she is; and so we were discussing as women are wont to do.

To this Celso said:

—Selvaggia was wrong, but she dislikes her for other reasons, for truly that young lady will always be considered beautiful by everybody, very beautiful. If she is not considered beautiful, I do not see another in Prato who could be called beautiful.

Then Selvaggia, who, if anything, is a little more bold than not, answered:

—There is no need to argue much about this because everyone has his own opinion, and some like dark-skinned women, and others fair-skinned ones. When it comes to us women, it is the same as at the cloth market, where one sells even the rough wool cloth and inexpensive floss silk.

—That is fine, Selvaggia,—Celso added,—but when one speaks of a beautiful woman, one means a woman who is generally liked by everyone, and not just by this man or that; for, though Tommaso likes his Nora beyond all measure, she is still as ugly as can be; and my neighbor, who was very beautiful, had a husband who could not stand her. It might be the humors,[5] which may or may not be compatible, or some other hidden reason. But one who is universally esteemed to be beautiful, as you are, must be universally liked by everyone, as you are, even though you yourself like few men, and I know it. It is certainly true that, in order to be perfectly beautiful, one needs many things, so much so that one finds few women who have even half of them.

Then Selvaggia said:

—These things are yours; you men, the world could not satisfy you. I once heard that a certain Momus,[6] who could find no other fault in Venus, criticized her slippers.

Verdespina then said:

—Now you see what mattered to him.

And Celso, laughing, added:

—And Stesichorus too, a very illustrious Sicilian poet, spoke badly of that Helen who, with her excessive beauty, moved a thousand Greek ships against the great kingdom of Troy.[7]

To this, Mona Lampiada immediately replied:

—Yes, but you can well see that he was struck blind for it and did not regain his sight until he retracted his words.

—And rightly so—continued Celso—for beauty and beautiful women, and beautiful women and beauty are worthy of praise and of everyone's esteem. For a beautiful woman is the most beautiful object one can admire, and beauty is the greatest gift God bestowed on His human creatures. And so, through her virtue we direct our souls to contemplation, and through contemplation to the desire for heavenly things. For this reason beautiful women have been sent among us as a sample and a foretaste of heavenly things, and they have such power and virtue that wise men have declared them to be the first and best object worthy of being loved. They have even called her the seat of love, the nest and abode of love, of that love, I say, which is the origin and source of all human joys.[8] One sees man forget himself for her, and, looking at a face adorned with this heavenly grace, his limbs shudder, his hair curls, he sweats and shivers at the same time, not unlike one who, unexpectedly seeing something divine, is possessed by divine frenzy, and when he is finally himself again, adores it with his thoughts and reveres it with his mind, and recognizing it as something like a god, gives himself to it as a sacrificial victim on the altar of the beautiful woman's heart.

To this Mona Lampiada said:

—Well then, Messer Celso, if you do not mind, do us a favor: tell us a little a bit about beauty and what constitutes a beautiful woman. These girls have been urging me for a while to ask you this, and I hesitated, but since you yourself have begun to speak about it, you have increased both my curiosity and my courage; and more so since I have heard that at the party my sister threw this past Carnival you spoke at such length about it with those ladies that my Mona Agnoletta talked of nothing else for many days thereafter. So, please, do us this favor. Besides, we have nothing else to do and with this light breeze we will while away the heat of the day more pleasantly than the other ladies who are playing or strolling in the garden.

To this, Celso answered:

—Yes, so that Selvaggia, as soon as she hears me say something not to her liking or not as fully as she would like, can say that I am speaking badly of women. But I take no greater pleasure than in praising them—and she has seen this many times herself, without ever thanking me for it. But let that be, since time will certainly change her white skin.[9]

Mona Lampiada then said:

—Don't worry, she won't say anything. So yes, please do us this favor.

And so, seeing them so eager, and so as not to be found wanting in politeness, he spoke to them in the manner you will hear if you read on.

For, not many days afterward, having asked him to repeat to me all that had been discussed, I wrote it all down on these pages as well as I could; and you must realize that many things said by both the ladies and by him are missing. After a few excuses, he began thus.

Celso: I have never refused any honorable request from a lady, nor do I wish to do so now. Let us then speak boldly about beauty in the midst of four very beautiful women. The first thing we must examine is what beauty is, in general. The second is the perfection, the purpose, or else the use of each particular part of the body, that is, of those parts that are kept uncovered. As Cicero pointed out,[10] Nature has arranged in her mysterious ways that those parts by which beauty can have its best effect should be situated in a prominent place, so as better to be seen by everyone. What is more, she quietly persuaded men and women to carry their upper parts uncovered and their lower parts covered because the first, as the proper seat of beauty, had to be seen, while for the others, it was not necessary since they are like a pedestal or base for the parts above them.

Mona Amorrorisca: Then preachers would be justified in reprimanding those people who cover their faces with masks because, according to you, that is the proper seat of beauty?

Celso: Yes, if they reprimanded only beautiful people who, truly, commit a great sin in masking so much beauty. But because they reprimand unattractive people as well, who should always go about masked, it seems to me they are not always correct. You can appreciate how displeasing ugliness can be from this: Alberto de' Bardi, from Vernia, whose excellent judgment we all know, says that when he sees Mona Ciona at a party, wearing that black satin she wears at all parties, the pleasure he derives from all the other beautiful women does not make up for the displeasure at seeing that one unattractive lady.

Mona Amorrorisca: Then, according to what you say, beauty does not reside in the feet, nor in the arms, nor in those parts of the body which are covered with clothes. But still, we do say: "Mona Bartolomea has beautiful legs. Apollonia has beautiful feet. Gemmetta has fine hips."

Celso: Even though Plato denied that beauty can reside in a single part and said that beauty seeks the union of different parts, as we will see in a short while,[11] still when we say that a single part is beautiful we mean that it is well-proportioned and that it is as it ought to be and fulfills its purpose. A finger, for example, should be smooth and white. We call such a finger beautiful, not because of the universal beauty philosophers demand, but because of its appropriate and particular beauty. All the same, when it comes to the arrangement of that beauty which, as if it were a deity, enraptures our sense of sight to the contemplation of itself and through the eyes binds the mind to the desire of such beauty which begins in the bosom and ends with the perfection of the face, to this, the lower parts of the body add nothing. They do, however, add to the shapeliness or beauty of the entire body, but clothed and covered as much as naked. And sometimes they do better when covered because, by being appropriately clothed, they become more charming. Therefore, we will speak primarily of the beauty of those parts that are not covered, and only in passing of those which are covered. Then we will see what elegance (*leggiadria*) consists of, what is charm (*vaghezza*), what we mean by grace (*grazia*) or by loveliness (*venustà*), what it is to have an air about you (*aria*) or not to have it, what is that quality which people call majesty (*maestà*) in you women, even though this is in some ways inappropriate. Our mind understands better the essence of things discussed when we offer examples, and rarely, in fact hardly ever, do all the parts that compose perfect and balanced beauty reside in one single woman. As Homer first said[12] and then that Carthaginian said to Hannibal: "The gods have not given every thing to everyone, but to some they have given intelligence, to others beauty, to many strength, to a few grace, and virtue to hardly anyone."[13] Thus I will take from each one of the four of you and will do like Zeuxis,[14] who chose the five most elegant girls of Croton and, taking from each her most exquisite feature, painted such a beautiful picture of Helen of Troy that in all of Greece one spoke of nothing else. The magnificent Messer Giovan Giorgio Trissino[15] probably learned portraiture from the same Zeuxis, or perhaps from Lucian,[16] who created his beautiful woman from the many beautiful parts he gathered from the best statues of the most renowned sculptors of his day. In the same way I will try to make, from four beautiful women, a perfect beauty. Well then, let us go on to the definition of beauty and to the true and essential understanding of it.

In his *Tusculanae,* Cicero says that beauty consists of a suitable arrangement of parts with a certain softness of color.[17] Others, one of whom was Aristotle, said it is a certain appropriate proportion arising from the manner in which differing parts go together one with the other.[18] Ficino, the

Platonist, in his work on the *Symposium,* in the second oration, says that beauty is a certain grace that comes from the concise union of several parts; and he uses the term concise because it implies a certain sweet and charming order, something akin to an elegant collective.[19] In his *Convivio,* which compared to the *Symposium* is a meager meal, Dante says that beauty is harmony.[20] Not so as to say something better than these men, but because when speaking with women it is necessary to speak a little more plainly, and not so as to define precisely but rather to explain, we will say that beauty is nothing else but ordered concord, akin to a harmony that arises mysteriously from the composition, union, and conjunction of several diverse and different parts that are, according to their own needs and qualities, differently well proportioned and in some way beautiful, and which, before they unite themselves into a whole, are different and discordant among themselves.

I have said concord and harmony as if they were similar, for just as in music the concordance of high, low, and other voices produces the beauty of vocal harmony, so too a stout limb, a thin one, a light one, a dark one, a straight one, a curved one, a little one, a big one, arranged and joined together by Nature in an inexplicable relationship, create that pleasing unity, that propriety, that moderation we call beauty. I say this is mysterious because we cannot explain why that white chin, those red lips, those black eyes, that wide hip, that little foot should produce, or arouse, or result in beauty. And yet, we see it is like this. If a woman were hairy, she would be ugly; if a horse were without hair, it would be a deformity. For a camel a hump is a thing of grace, for a woman, a misfortune. This can only come from a mysterious order in Nature that, in my opinion, the human intellect cannot fathom. But the eye, which has been appointed by Nature herself as the judge in this case, esteeming itself to be so, forces us to accept its sentence without appeal.

I have said different because, as I have just said, beauty is a concord and union of diverse things, just as the hand of a musician, the intent that moves that hand, the bow, the viol, and the strings are things different and diverse one from the other and yet produce the sweetness of harmony, so too the face is different from the bosom, and the bosom from the neck, and the arms from the legs, but arranged and joined together in one person by the mysterious intentions of Nature they give birth, as if it were inevitable, to beauty. What Cicero says about the delicacy of color seems to me superfluous because every time the specific parts that produce such beauty are themselves beautiful, well formed, and perfectly arranged, composed, and proportioned, they will of necessity color the body they are thus making up with the delicacy of color it needs for its own true perfection. For, just as in a body whose humors are well balanced and whose parts well arranged one finds health, and health produces a bright and lively complexion that outwardly reveals its presence within the body, so too the perfection of each specific part united in the creation of the whole will spread the color necessary for the perfect union and harmonious beauty of the entire body.

Plutarch writes that Alexander the Great gave off, from his limbs, a most delicate fragrance, and attributes this to nothing other than the good balance, or rather, the perfect balance of his humors and his entire complexion.[21] Thus, to return to our proposition, the cheeks must be fair (*candido*). Fair is a color that, besides being white, also has a certain luster, as ivory does; while white is that which does not glow, such as snow. If the cheeks, then, in order to be called beautiful, need to be fair, and the bosom needs only to be white, and since the creation of complete beauty requires the perfect beauty of each part, it will be necessary that each has the right color, that is, the color that is necessary to its own particular beauty or essence. Having that color on their own, it will follow that each part will also have it in union with the other; and, having it, it will inevitably spread that delicacy of color as is necessary. There ought not to be an abundance of different colors in one and the same part, but a different color in different parts, according to the variety and needs of these different parts; somewhere white, as in the hands, somewhere fair and vermillion, as in the cheeks, somewhere black, as in the eyelashes, somewhere red, as in the lips, somewhere blonde, as in the hair. This then, my ladies, is not the definition, but an exposition of the definitions of beauty.

Mona Lampiada: Forgive me if I should sometimes bother you with a question, but I am one of those women who, granted that they be ignorant, nonetheless wish to learn something every time they are given the opportunity. When you speak of beauty in general, are you referring to men or to women, or are you speaking of one and the other interchangeably?

Celso: It is a great sign of knowledge to begin to realize that one does not know and wishes to know. Thus Socrates, who was declared a wise man by the Oracle of Apollo, used to say that, for all his great pains and studies, he had learned nothing else than the realization that he did not know.[22] However, you do not say this because you do not know, but rather on account of your natural modesty. And you ask not so that I might teach you, for you know more than I do, but for the sake of these other ladies who, being a little younger, have less experience than you.

I say, therefore, in answer to your question, that if you had read the oration Aristophanes recited in Plato's *Symposium*,[23] there would be no need for me now to clarify this matter, nor if you had read certain fine passages by Monsignor Bembo in his youth.[24] I am tempted to tell you the entire story, were it not for the fact that it would take too long, and so I will save it for another time.

Mona Lampiada: Oh, please, do tell us now, for time is on our hands. Another day we may not have the opportunity.

Celso: Since you would like me to, I will tell you, but as briefly as possible for, if I were to tell it exactly as it is written, we would be here till evening.

When Jove created the first men and the first women, he made them with duplicate sets of limbs, that is, with four arms, four legs, two heads. And thus, being double, they had twice the strength. And there were three types of persons: some were male on both sides, some were female, and these were few, and the rest, which were the majority, were male on one side and female on the other. Now it happened that these people thus formed were unappreciative of the gifts received from Jove and even considered taking over Paradise from him. Hearing about this, Jove set aside all other advice and, unwilling to destroy completely the human race lest there should then be no one left to adore him and thus deprive him of his position, decided to cleave them all in half through the middle and to make two people out of each one, for he thought that by thus dividing them in two their strength and daring would also be divided. So, without further ado, Jove carried out his decision and arranged matters so that we were left as you see us nowadays. Mercury was the sawyer,[25] and Aesculapius the master encharged with repairing us and healing our breast,[26] which suffered more than any of our other parts (and which, for you, Selvaggia, he certainly fixed far too well), and with mending all the other parts the saw had damaged. And so, as you see, everyone is left either male or female, except for a few individuals who escaped and ran so much they completely ruined themselves and were never again good for anything and were called Hermaphrodites, which derives from Hermes, that is, Mercury, and means "escaped from Mercury."[27]

Those who were male in both halves, or are descended from those who were, wishing to return to their original state, seek their other half, which was another male. They thus love and admire each other's beauty, some virtuously, as Socrates loved the handsome Alcibiades,[28] or as Achilles loved Patroclus,[29] or Nisus loved Euryalus;[30] and some unchastely, as certain wicked men, more unworthy of any name or fame than that man who, in order to gain fame, set fire to the temple of the Ephesian goddess.[31] And all these men, both the virtuous and the wicked, generally flee the company of you ladies. And I know very well that you are familiar with some of these even in our own day.

Those who were female in both halves, or are descended from those who were, love each other's beauty, some in purity and holiness, as the elegant Laudomia Forteguerra loves the most illustrious Margaret of Austria,[32] some lasciviously, as in ancient times Sappho from Lesbos[33] and in our own times in Rome the great prostitute Cecilia Venetiana.[34] This type of woman by nature spurns marriage and flees from intimate conversation with us men. And, we must believe, these women are those who willingly become nuns and willingly remain so, and they are few, because the majority of women are kept in monasteries by force and live there in despair.

The third type, those who were male and female, and who were the majority, are those from whom you are descended, you who have a husband and hold him dear, as Alcestis, the wife of King Admetus,[35] and others who would not refuse to die for their husbands' sake. In short, they are all those women who look upon the face of a man eagerly but chastely and as sacred law allows. And it is we men who either have a wife or are looking for one. In short, it is those who like nothing more than the beautiful face of you ladies, those who, in order to be reunited with their other half and rejoice in its beauty, would not spurn any danger, as Orpheus for his dear Eurydice[36] and the Roman nobleman Caius Gracchus for his beloved Cornelia,[37] and as I would do for that cruel lady who, unwilling to admit she is my other half and I am hers, flees from me as if I were a strange creature.

Verdespina: If I may tell you, you let yourself be so little understood, with this love of yours, it would not be a surprise if the woman you love and claim to be your other half, as one ought to say, does not know of it, and therefore does not do you those respectable favors a gentle lady should do for a virtuous man such as yourself. Yet, there is not a person in Prato who does not believe you are in love. Just a few days ago, I heard someone inquire about it with great insistence, and everyone said they thought so, but did not know with whom. And when I consider the things you sometimes say, such as, "She who has me does not know it, and she who knows it does not have me," I am convinced of my first opinion, that the lady you love does not know it, and the lady you do not love thinks you love her. Nevertheless, you are so secretive about it, one does not know very well who is the one that you feign to love, and the one you really do love.

Celso: Gentle Verdespina, do you think I am so base in spirit and so forgetful of myself as to have closed my heart completely to Love's arrows? I too am a man, I too seek to find my other half, I too seek to enjoy the beauty of she who has been placed in front of me as the radiant object of my fortunate eyes and as the consolation of my intellect. But I enjoy her silently and on my own, since the end of my love, which is pure and chaste, having planted its roots on ground cultivated by virtue, is contentment itself with the sight of my lady which cannot be denied to me by any accident because, when she is hidden from my corporeal eye, she is visible to the eye of my intellect. Therefore, even if my lady were to hide herself from me as she wished, I would always see her, always admire her, always rejoice in her and be content. And when I complain about her, I am talking idly, for truly I have no cause to complain whatsoever, for I desire nothing from her which I could not have, even against her will. Perhaps a time will come when she who has me will know it, and she who does not have me will find out.

Let us now return to the severed men and the divided women; unfortunately, we have wandered away from home. We will say that there is no need to discuss the first type, nor the second since they either contemplate the beauty of their own kind divinely and in virtue or wickedly and in vice. We cannot speak of the first because our intellect, while it resides in this prison, is scarcely able to consider divine things. About the wicked and depraved, God forbid that one should talk of such dreary offspring[38] in the company of chaste and virtuous women such as yourselves. We are left, then, to talk about you and about us, that is, about men who love women and women who love men, but who do so courteously and chastely and who are enflamed and enlightened by a virtuous ray, as has been said several times. But it seems to me Selvaggia is making fun of this.

Selvaggia: I am not making fun of this; on the contrary, I am eager to see what conclusion you will draw from all this.

Celso: I wish to draw this conclusion, that, since each of us desires with a natural instinct and appetite to rejoin and be reunited with his other half and become complete once again, it is inevitable that she should appear beautiful to us and, since she appears beautiful, it is inevitable that we love her, because true love, according to what the entire Platonist school claims, is nothing else but a desire for beauty. Loving her, it is inevitable that we should seek her out; seeking her, that we should find her (who could hide anything from the eyes of a true lover?); finding her, that we should contemplate her; contemplating her, that we should rejoice in her; rejoicing in her, that we should receive from her an incomprehensible pleasure, for pleasure is the end of all human action.[39] In fact, it is that highest good so sought after by philosophers. In my opinion, speaking of earthly things, it is not found anywhere else but here. Therefore, it will no longer seem so remarkable that a gentle lady and a worthy man, burning with the fire of love (which is the only light that, through the eyes, opens our intellect and shows us our other half), should undertake any labor, should expose themselves to any danger, in order to find oneself again in someone else, and someone else in oneself. And so, in conclusion, so as not to hold you in suspense any longer, we must say that it is appropriate for a lady to contemplate the beauty of a man, and for a man that of a lady. And so, when we speak of beauty in general, we mean both yours and ours. Nevertheless, since a more delicate and particular beauty resides more in you, diffuses itself more in you, and in you is more discernible on account of your complexion, which is much more delicate and softer than ours, and, as many sages rightly claim, it has been made by Nature so gentle, so soft, so sweet, so lovable, so desirable, so admirable and so delightful, so that it would be a rest, a refreshment, even a harbor and a destination and a refuge in the course of all human labors, for this reason, leaving behind today all talk of male beauty, my entire discussion, my entire discourse, all my thoughts will be devoted to the beauty of you ladies. And if anyone wants to reproach me for it, let him do so, for I profess, not on my own, but in line with the conclusions not only of natural philosophers, but also of some theologians, that your beauty is evidence of heavenly things, an image and a semblance of the treasures of Heaven. How could earthly man ever be satisfied with the idea that our blessedness, which ought to consist above all in always contemplating the omnipotent essence of God and to rejoice in our vision of His divinity, could be continual blessedness without any hint of satiety, if he could not see that to contemplate the gracefulness of a beautiful woman, to rejoice in her elegance, to feast his eyes on her pleasant beauty, is an incomprehensible pleasure, an indescribable blessedness, a sweetness which, when it is over, would like to begin again, a happiness that makes him forget himself and transcend himself? And so, my dear men of Prato, if sometimes I look upon these women of yours a little too attentively, do not take it badly. Do you know what Petrarch said to Laura?

If you were less beautiful, I would be less bold.[40]

Do you think that, when I look at them, I take them away from you? Have no such fear, for I do them no harm whatsoever. I do it only in order to learn how to enjoy the treasures of Heaven, for my behavior is not so bad that I may not hope to get there. And so as not to get there and look like a country bumpkin the first time he goes into town, and so as not to have to learn how to contemplate beautiful things, I am becoming accustomed to it down here, with these beautiful faces, the best I can. And if anyone wants to reproach me for this, let him do so, for I forgive him. And I do believe it is a very fine revenge not to be able to be justly reproached. And I know very well that he who has a foul stomach cannot help but show it in his breath. There you see how far I have been carried by my righteous indignation.

Mona Amorrorisca: Well, now, Messer Celso, no more. Although it is fine for a gentle heart to bear some righteous indignation, nonetheless, letting oneself be carried away by it is neither elegant nor courteous.

Celso: Certainly the indignation is great, especially against the one who, without reason, moved against me. But you ladies are the reason for this, since they tear my reputation to shreds for speaking willingly about you, praising you, defending you from the barkings of these fools (who, by speaking badly of you, want to be considered your lovers), writing honorably of you, and showing myself to be your advocate. But, my ladies, let them say what they wish, for I wish to look upon you, to love you, to speak of you, to write about you, to serve you, and to adore you. And to prove to you, my dear ladies, that what I have promised you in words I will attain in deeds, I say that from the previous discussion which concluded that we are the other half of each other, one draws the irrefutable conclusion that you women are as noble as we men, as wise, as apt in learning, be it moral or speculative, as skilled in mechanical arts and knowledge as we, and those same powers and possibilities that are in our spirit are also in yours, because, when a complete whole is divided into two parts equally, it is inevitable that one part be equal to the other, as good as the other, as beautiful as the other. And so, with this argument and this conclusion, I will boldly say to your and my enemies who, when they are in front of you seem to die for you and then, behind your back, speak badly about you, that you are in all things and at all times our equals, even though sometimes this is not universally apparent on account of the domestic duties and house-hold management which you have modestly assumed in caring for the family. And in the same way we see that between the philosopher and the craftsman, the doctor and the merchant, there is a very great difference with respect to the operations of the intellect. But there is no need to discuss this at the moment, for we have wandered far too far from our subject.

Still, I wanted to warn you about something. If someone should say to you that that story about splitting in two is a campfire story,[41] you should answer that Plato told it and that it is a story that was narrated one night by a wise philosopher[42] at one of Plato's parties. If they be intelligent men, this answer will refute them; if they be ignorant men, they will be malicious anyway, and you should think very little of them, for a malicious spirit is incapable of wisdom. To say that it is one of Plato's stories indicates that it is full of high and divine mysteries and that it is meant to symbolize what I have told you, that is, that we are one and the same thing, one and the same perfection, and that you must seek us and love us, and we must seek and love you, and you are nothing without us, and we are nothing without you, our perfection is in you, and yours in us, to say nothing of the thousands of other beautiful mysteries which, for the moment, we need not go into. Do not forget to say that it was Plato; keep that well in mind.

Since I have shown you, as far as I could, what beauty in general is, I am now left, according to my promise, with the task of showing you the beauty of individual parts and their perfection. It is in these parts, as I mentioned before, that God has placed, with wonderful order, the preser-vation of the entire composition, for each part helps the other parts, and each part uses the strengths (*virtù*) of the other parts.

And, first of all, it seems appropriate to me to speak of the carriage, that is the shape of the entire person, which almighty God, who created us to His own end and so that we should contemplate His heavenly order, turned and lifted up toward the heavens.[43] The form of other animals, which were created for the benefit of humanity or for the beauty and adornment of the universe, the Almighty turned toward the earth so that with their eyes they should gaze upon it as their end and with their lowered forelegs they should always crawl upon it on all fours. To humanity how-ever, He granted an upright carriage, the ability to turn his eyes to the sky and keep them forever fixed upon the virtues of those higher beauties which, when this prison will be opened,[44] will, by the grace of God, be his reward, his hostel, his rest after earthly labors. This same man, nonetheless, as we have said, while he travels on this earthly journey, occasionally refreshes himself and rests, he restores himself and gathers strength, my beautiful ladies, from your sweet beauty, just like a tired pilgrim at an inn, until he reaches his desired destination.

The carriage or form of a man can be contained in a square, since a man, when he extends his arms to form a cross, is as long from the tip of his middle finger in one hand to the tip of his middle finger in the other, as he is from the sole of his feet to the tip of his head, which is popularly called the crown. This figure should be at least nine heads long, that is, nine times the length from the lowest part of the chin to the tip of the head. Others have displayed it within a perfect circle by drawing lines through the genitals, which they claim to be the center of our figure, to the circumference, that is, in this way.[45]

Mona Lampiada: Let us move over a little this way, where it is flatter and cleaner. It will be easier for you to draw. And while you are at it, draw the figure in the square as well, showing the width and height.

Celso: Here it is.

Selvaggia: Since you have done so well, show us also the drawing of a man in a circle.

Celso: Here you are, since nothing can be denied to you.

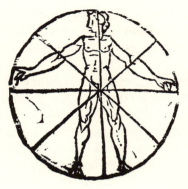

See how the lines, which are all the same length out from the middle, form the circumference I mentioned.

Now we come to the head, which I will draw for you as best I can, for this is not at all my profession, though it would not be unsuitable for anyone with a lofty mind. On the contrary, it would do one great credit for, among the Greeks, painting was counted among the liberal arts.[46]

You can see, then, that in order to measure exactly the height of the head (and note that I call head everything from the top of the neck up), one must draw a straight line that must rest on top of another straight line that comes out from the lowest part of the chin, and must go and meet another straight line that comes out from the top of the head; and the height of a man who is reasonably shaped and well proportioned both in height and width will be nine times the length of that line. And what we say about men, we always understand to be the same for women, be it in this or any other measurement. Still, there have been many learned and worthy men

who have written that women, for the most part, do not exceed seven
heads; others have written that in order to be well proportioned they must
not exceed seven-and-a-half.[47] And I think the common practice of Nature
lends support to their opinion.

And so you see that one takes the measurement for the entire person
from the head, and the measurement for the head from the entire person.
And since a body of the proper height, and especially that of a woman,
should not exceed seven-and-a-half spans, a span is nine fingers high (that
is, the span and fingers of a well-proportioned hand), therefore a proper
and well formed head will be seven-and-a-half fingers high.

And since we have started drawing, I want to show you how painters
schematize the perfect profile as a triangle. But remember, very few women
turn out well in profile. One of the most perfect profiles I think I have seen
to date here in Prato belongs to that gentle country-girl who lives at the
Three Canals.[48] And the girl from Marcatale,[49] who has such a pretty face
among ugly ones, who has that beautiful expression, and who was so well
liked in the comedy that was performed at the house of the Villani,[50] and
who all of Prato rightfully judged most beautiful, has an imperfect profile
because of a tiny little imperfection in the proportions of her face. Very few
people notice this because, as the saying goes, "Not every bull can read."[51]
Still, she has a pleasant girlish air. Now, here is the drawing of the triangle.

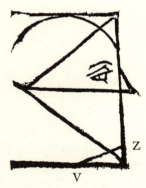

These painters say that one should draw a straight line from the angle,
the same length as the sides of the triangle. Going up from the end of that
line one should draw the nose. A finger and a half from the angle, or a little
more, on this side of the same line, one should place the ear, letting that
point which, narrowing like a small balas ruby,[52] brings the ear to such a
graceful conclusion at its lower end, fall under this line.

From the upper corner, they then draw another straight line, the same length as the middle one. From this line they drop a curved line down to the side of the triangle. This soft and sweet curve, falling to the top of the nose, which must be against the inner corner of the eye, follows the curve of the head toward the forehead, and from the forehead to the top of the nose in that little hollow between the eyebrows.

From the lower corner they draw a horizontal line and it ends directly under the ear. One quarter of the way in, where you see the letter *V,* they draw a line that is nearly semicircular. One part of this line ends a little above the angle at the letter *Z,* where the chin ends, and the other part meets the beginning of the throat. And this shows how the chin should have a little bulge underneath, just like Amelia's cousin, whose pretty little face gains a great deal of gracefulness from it.

And there is as much distance from the tip of the chin to the top of the upper lip as from the top of the nose to the hairline, which is the end of the forehead. And there is as much distance from the top of the upper lip to the beginning of the nose as from the inner corner of the eye to the middle of the bridge of the nose. The base of the nose must be as wide as it is long. The hollow of the eye, from the eyebrow to the cheek, must be as wide as its length from the nose to where it ends near the ear.

There are many other measurements which, because they matter little and Nature rarely uses them, we will leave to painters who, with a brush-stroke more or less, can lengthen or shorten as they see fit.

Mona Amorrorisca: Dear me, you have utterly confused me with all your measurements. So then, when we make babies, either little boys or little girls, we would need a yardstick and a compass. To tell you the truth, if I ever thought I was beautiful—and many times I have been told so, and sometimes, looking into the mirror, I must confess I believed it, and even thought it quite true—from now on in truth I will think I am deformed. Oh my, I don't think I have any of these proportions, and so I must go and hide myself.

Celso: But there is no need to rush into hiding. Given all the aspects of true and measured beauty, even though you do not possess them all completely, it suffices that you have enough of them that, in the opinion of others, you are worthy of being considered more on the beautiful side. And if that absolutely perfect harmony is not born from the concord of your parts, it suffices that it is born with enough grace and enough beauty so that there is no reason for you to go into hiding, but rather to show yourself more than you do. And your handsome little sons and elegant little daughters will attest to it to all those people who will not have had opportunity to admire you, for all your features are reflected in your children.

Mona Amorrorisca: Well then, if Nature may have failed me in some little part, you supplement it so fully with your words that I can easily return to my first opinion. But let us not waste time with such chatter. Please, do continue your discourse.

Celso: Since you wish it, it will be done. Let us then return to expound on the particular aspects of the face, and then we will discuss the other members, each in its turn.

First the eyes, in which the noblest and most perfect of all the senses resides, through which our intellect gathers, as through windows of transparent glass, everything visible. And furthermore, since through the eyes our faculties are known better than through any of the other senses,[53] we must, therefore, believe that Nature made them with great skill. As a result, since they examine the universe, she placed them in the highest part of the body so that from here they could fulfill their office with greater ease.[54] She made them round so that, given the shape that is the most comprehensive of all,[55] sight could more fully take in the objects that presented themselves to it. Nature realized there was another advantage in this, namely that such a spherical shape, not impeded by any type of corner, can look in all directions and turn in whichever direction it likes more easily. This variability is further aided by that pure liquid that keeps the eyes constantly wet, for you know very well that from wetness comes lubrication, and all things move and turn more easily on a lubricant than on a dry surface.[56]

She placed at their center, like two sparks of fire, the pupils, popularly called lights, with which the power of sight, actually located here, seizes the objects that appear in front of them. There is no need to discuss whether the eye seeks the object or whether the object seeks the eye, for this is not a question pertinent to our present inquiry.

Through this roundness, therefore, the mind, knowing itself, is sometimes forced to reveal the secret thoughts of the heart, for often one reads in the eyes what is written in the heart. The sight in each eye joins with the other in such a way that, without hindering one another, they can gaze upon an object both at the same time, and when the right eye looks at something, the left does not look at something else.[57]

Leonardo da Vinci, *Mona Lisa* (Paris, Louvre; courtesy of Alinari/Art Resource, NY). "*. . . for often one reads in the eyes what is written in the heart.*"

And so that they may be well equipped and protected from any danger of something falling from the forehead, such as sweat or other things, she strengthened them with the hair of the eyebrows, like two embankments that would withstand every attack. She covered them with two movable eyelids, easy to open and close, they too strengthened with hair that would prevent anything from flying inadvertently into them. The continual movement of the eyelids, which lower and raise with incredible speed, not only does not hinder the power of sight, but gives it strength and rest. And when they are tired and they hold within them peaceful slumber, they hide the eyes much to the great peacefulness and marvelous sweetness of all the other members. The sharpness of sight, placed as it were in transparent parchment, is strengthened and sustained in its clarity by virtue of the liquid I have already mentioned. Experience plainly shows this, for as you know, as soon as the eye, for whatever reason, dries out, it immediately loses its power of sight.

The nose begins at the edge of the eyebrows and ends above the mouth, along the space we drew for you before. Rising slightly, it seems to mark the boundary between one eye and the other, or even to be a bastion between them. And the cheeks, one on this side and one on the other, rising with that soft swelling of theirs, seem to stand in defense of those same eyes. But, to return to the nose, we say that the upper portion is made of solid matter and the lower portion of something like cartilage, very soft and flexible so that it can more easily be handled and kept clean, and when it is hit, which is easily done, for it protrudes so much, it is not damaged very much because it bends with the blow. Inside this member, which may appear to be of little importance, reside three important functions: breathing, smelling, and purging the brain through its little cavities.[58] The great Maker placed these very useful and important functions in this part in such a way that it seems to have been made more for the beauty and ornament of the face than for the uses I have just mentioned.

Under the nose there is the mouth, with two functions: one is to speak, the other to send nourishment to the appropriate places. The mouth, cleft lengthwise, was then hemmed by Nature with two lips that seem to be of finest coral, like the edges of a most beautiful fountain. The Ancients consecrated them to beautiful Venus, for this is the seat of those loving kisses capable of letting souls pass mutually from the body of one to that of the other lover. And, therefore, when we gaze intently upon the lips, filled with extreme pleasure, we feel our soul always about to leave us, eager to go and rest herself upon them.

There is no need to discuss the palate and the tongue because they must not be seen, but we will speak about the teeth which, besides their usefulness in chewing food and starting in the mouth the process of digestion, and helping the food pass more easily to the stomach, bestow so much beauty, so much grace, so much charm to a pleasant face that, without them, sweetness does not seem to reside too willingly upon it.

What else? If the teeth are not beautiful, laughter cannot be beautiful. Laughter, if used well, at the right time and with modesty, turns the mouth into Paradise. Moreover, it is a most sweet messenger of the peace and tranquility of the heart, for wise men claim laughter is nothing more than radiance from the serenity of the soul. And thus, if we are to believe Plato in his *Republic*[59] (which I, for one, do), it is appropriate for noble and gentle ladies, as an indication of their happiness, to laugh with modesty, with restraint, with honesty, with little bodily movement and a low tone, and rarely rather than frequently, as does Selvaggia's sister-in-law, whom you were discussing just a little while ago.[60]

Verdespina: And your godmother,[61] who often laughed, was admired for that laughter more than for all her other fine qualities, which were so many that she rightfully stood first among all the ladies in Prato.

Celso: My godmother had such a charming laugh that whenever she laughed she always pleased, but this is not so with everyone. Your Amaretta, who is even more pretty when she laughs, if she were to laugh too often would not be as pleasing. And yet she has very beautiful teeth. But these are among those charms the heavens rarely bestow down here, and they fall upon few people. Therefore laughter should be rare, especially since excessive laughter is a sign of too much happiness, and too much happiness is not appropriate to a rational person.

Now Nature, knowing how a little border around the bottom would give bare teeth much gracefulness, and how much charm if she divided them with a small but well-measured space, tied them together with the gums, as if with a bit of ribbon, and separated them with that space measured with the compass of Mistress Nature so that they would provide not only utility but also that pleasure that you and I have tasted a thousand times, and will continue to savor as long as Mona Amorrorisca will consent to show us her teeth.

Selvaggia: Now there, Mona Amorrorisca, do not cover them up. On feastdays one uncovers holy objects, one does not hide them away.

Mona Amorrorisca: Go ahead, all of you, and tease me. You know, Selvaggia, there's something for everyone. So, please, do continue.

Celso: The chin begins from the cheeks, in a gentle line, and ends in those two little hills which seem to place between them a very sweet little hollow, as in the case of Appollonia, who you said the other day looked so beautiful the morning of Corpus Christi at San Domenico's.[62] If I am to tell you my opinion, she is a beautiful and graceful young woman, with few to equal her in this town. A beautiful jewel tied to a worthless ring. May God be with her.[63]

The ears then open out from the highest part of the body so that they may more easily gather the sounds that fall from the air that reverberates within them. They are bare so that sound may enter them more easily. They have folds and winding turns so that sounds that enter them may not, on account of the difficult path, turn around and go back out.[64] And they are made a little like that small instrument you call a funnel which, gathering and condensing a fluid, makes it go through a small channel into a larger vessel so that none is spilled. In the same manner, the ear, gathering scattered sounds through a small little channel, diffuses them into the greater vessel of the intellect, to be stored in the memory, which is located in the occipital lobe, which we Tuscans call the scruff of the neck.

They are not made of soft or weak or flabby skin, as we see in many other animals, for you can well imagine that they would have been very deformed. They were not strengthened with hard and solid bones, for these would make hearing more difficult than not. Moreover, they would have hindered rest for the entire body, because the hardness and rigidity of those bones would not have allowed us to rest our head upon them in the silence of sleep or in the repose from bodily fatigue, as we often do. Therefore, they were moulded in a material that tended toward softness but not flabbiness, that in times of rest would not be of hindrance, and that was capable of gathering sounds.

Putting aside their usefulness for the sake of their beauty, one ought to look at that semicircle or reddish border with that pendant tip, like a balas ruby, as we said.[65] How beautiful, how charming, how graceful it is! And if, as is the custom in many parts of Italy, one hangs a precious jewel from it, not only does the ear by comparison not lose gracefulness, but on the contrary gains from it and the jewel suffers the loss.

In that hole that sends the sound inside, the ears have those certain folds and winding turns and so on in the form of a screw, as we have said, so that sounds my pass more slowly through such difficult paths and so give the sense of hearing time to reiterate them to the common sense,[66] and also so as to make it difficult for little animals to fly inside. But if one should enter, it finds in there a certain sticky matter that holds it back from going on to the end and hindering the use of hearing. Those tortuous paths, carved out like little caverns, serve also to magnify sound inside them, as in the folds of a horn, or a seashell, or in the loops of a trumpet, or as one sees all day long in the caverns, caves, and deep valleys out in the country where sounds become wrapped up, double in volume, and resound.

Then comes the throat, capable of bending and turning on all sides with great charm. It also covers and protects the two vital canals, called tubes, which breathe and send the food that has been ground up by the mouth down to the pot of the stomach to cook.

The shoulders slope from under it, and they give way to the arms, with the bend of the elbow, and with the admirable and necessary use of the hands, the most eminent ministers of the sense of touch. With their concave palm and the flexibility of their fingers, they are capable of picking up and holding whatever they like. In the end it is difficult to decide what is greater, their usefulness or their beauty.

The breadth of the bosom lends great majesty to the entire body. The breasts are here, like two hills filled with snow and roses,[67] with two little crowns of fine spouts at the top, like drinking straws for that beautiful and useful vessel.[68] Besides their usefulness in distilling nourishment for little babies, the breasts have a certain splendor, with such a novel charm, that we are forced to rest our eyes upon them in spite of ourselves, rather, to our great pleasure, as I do, looking at the most candid breasts of one of you . . . Here we go, covering up the altars! If you do not rearrange that veil the way it was before, I will proceed no further.

Mona Lampiada: Come now, put it away, Selvaggia, you have worn us out by now. There, you did well to take it off your neck. You see? That's how it's done. Now then, Messer Celso, do continue with your oration, for the sacred relics have been unveiled.[69]

Celso: I believe it is proper to keep silent about the other parts down to the legs (as was said before, they are kept covered and do not give anything to our beauty except in their totality). We will then speak only of the legs, by whose motion we move from place to place by bending the knees and their corresponding tendons from the hips to the heels. They are, in fact, bound

Raphael, *La Fornarina* (Rome, Galleria Nazionale; courtesy of Alinari/Art Resource, NY). *"The breasts are . . . like two hills filled with snow and roses, with two little crowns of fine spouts at the top."*

to the base of the entire body, that is, the feet. Being the beginning and base of all the other limbs, the feet are worthy of much attention and very important for the total beauty of the entire body because every time the eyes are tired, or rather, every time they are amazed and astonished by the overflowing and incomprehensible sweetness they have received from contemplating the eyes, the cheeks, the mouth, and the other parts, curtailing their power of sight within themselves, they seem to fall as if afraid and come to rest on the feet, not unlike a tired head that falls to rest on a pillow. And so, my dear ladies, do not be too stingy about showing them sometimes. Learn from Roman women, who take as much care of their feet as of their faces.

It should suffice for now to have spoken of the beauty, utility, purpose, reason, artistry, and proportion of all parts in general. When we come to compose a beautiful woman, we will speak more precisely by using you as examples.

Verdespina: If Diambra were present at these discourses of yours, oh, I can tell you very well, she would swell with rage. She thinks herself a new Helen of Troy for no other reason (though she considers herself beautiful in every way) than the clarity of her hair. She is wont to say that regardless of how beautiful a woman thinks she is, if she does not have beautiful hair, her beauty is despoiled of every grace and every splendor. And you have not even mentioned it.

Celso: She has a very good point, and you did well to remind me, for I had forgotten the hair for the very good reason that it seems to me that ladies from these parts hold it in little esteem, and even brides keep it covered. Except for her, I have not seen many ladies who let their hair blow in the wind. This is a bad thing, for hair is a great ornament of beauty and was created by Nature for the evaporation of superfluous matter from the brain and other parts of the head.[70] Even though each hair is very thin, it has holes in it so that it may exude the superfluous matter I have mentioned. As for a discussion of its specific beauty, and what Apuleius said about it when he described his Photis,[71] I will wait until we come to composing our imaginary woman.

Now, having discussed almost enough about beauty, we are still left with stating what elegance is, and then we will have fulfilled our promise.

According to some, and to what the word itself says, elegance (*leggiadria*) is nothing more than the observance of an unspoken law,[72] given and promulgated by Nature to you ladies for the movement, bearing, and use both of your entire body and of your specific limbs with grace, modesty, gentility, measure, style, so that no movement, no gesture be without moderation, without manner, without measure, without intention, but rather, as this unspoken law obliges us, it be trimmed, composed, regulated, graceful.[73] Because this law is not written down anywhere but in a certain natural judgment which of itself neither knows nor can explain the reason, except to say that Nature wants it like this, I have called it unspoken. And furthermore, because books cannot teach this law, nor practice illustrate it, it is not generally observed by all beautiful women. In fact, one sees all day long many of them so ill-mannered, so affected, it is a nuisance to look upon them. And that gentle Lucrezia, who lives toward San Domenico, because she is a faithful observer of this law and has all those elegant traits one looks for, is well-liked by everyone. And even though her features may be lacking in some little way according to the standards of scrupulous draftsmen, nonetheless if she laughs she is pleasing, if she speaks she is delightful, if she remains silent she fills others with admiration, if she walks she is graceful, if she sits she is charming, if she sings she is sweet, if she dances Venus is in her company, if she converses the Muses are teaching her. In short, she does everything marvelously.

Mona Lampiada: You did not know how much I like this young lady, not only because she has a good character, as you yourself know, but also because I think she is beautiful, and so I am pleased we share the same opinion.

Celso: She is certainly a pleasure. But do you know who I also thought was always a gentle young girl and adorned with so much elegance and so much charm that if I had to paint a Venus I do not know what other woman but her I would portray? And do not think I say this because of that marvelous mind, or that grand manner of hers, for today it is not my intention to speak of beauty of the soul. I say it only because of the beauty of her body.

Selvaggia: Who is she, God save you from all harm?[74]

Celso: If God save me, therefore, from your sharp looks, I say Quadrabianca Buonvisa seems to me to be an elegant and pleasant young girl, and it seems to me she is quite attractive.[75]

Selvaggia: A grace the heavens grant in abundance to few,[76] and indeed you tell the truth.

Celso: Yes, and you are among those few. But grace is another thing I wanted to talk about with you, that grace that is part of beauty, not of those who are handmaidens to Venus.[77] Metaphorically, those Graces signify nothing more than the combined rewards given by grateful people in return for benefits already received. Because in affairs of the heart and matters of love many benefits accumulate between the lovers, and they reward each other for them, all day long, the Graces were assigned as servants to beautiful Venus.[78] Leaving aside the other two, we can take Aglaïa, who signifies splendor.[79] She will do very well for us, for in our opinion grace is nothing more than a splendor which is awakened in some mysterious way by a special union of parts, so that we cannot say, "It is these parts, it is those parts," that are brought together, joined, and arranged together with every consummate beauty, or rather perfection. This splendor strikes our eyes with such keenness on their part, with such satisfaction for the heart and pleasure for the mind, that they are immediately obliged quietly to turn our desire to those sweet rays. And thus, as we have mentioned before, many times we see a face whose features do not adhere to the standard measurements for beauty, yet spreads that splendor of grace of which we spoke. Such is the case with Modestina who, although she is not as tall and well proportioned as I mentioned earlier, nonetheless has so much grace in that pretty little face of hers that everyone likes her. On the other hand, one will see a woman with well-proportioned features who could rightfully be considered beautiful by everyone, and, nevertheless, will not have that certain deliciousness, as is the case with the sister of Mona Ancilia. Thus we must believe this splendor comes from a mysterious proportion and from a measure that is not in our books, which we do not know, nor even imagine, and is, as we say for those things we cannot express, a *je ne sais quoi*. To say it is a ray of love, or some other such quintessential thing, though this be learned, subtle, and ingenious, nonetheless, does not reflect the truth.

It is called grace because it makes the woman on whom this ray shines, in whom this mysterious proportion is diffused, grateful, that is, appreciated; as do the graces given for benefits received, that make he who gives them feel grateful and appreciated.

And this is all I wish to or am able to say for now. If you want to know more, gaze into the eyes of that clear light that shines with those most beautiful eyes of hers upon every wandering intellect that goes seeking the splendor of grace.

In order to explain what charm (*vaghezza*) is,[80] you must first know what it really is, for the word "charm" really means three things: first, movement from place to place, as Petrarch well demonstrates:

Bring your wandering [*vaghi*] thoughts to a better place.[81]

Second, desire, as the same author says:

I am so desirous [*vago*] to gaze upon her.[82]

Boccaccio, in the *Fiammetta* says: "of that which they had become desirous [*vaghi*]."[83]

Third, beautiful. Again Petrarch wrote:

The beautiful [*vaghi*] behavior and angelic manners.[84]

And Boccaccio in the same book: "a crowd of beautiful [*vaghe*] young women."[85]

From the first meaning, that is, movement, we derive the word vagabond (*vagabondo*), and from vagabond, that is, a man who wanders, we derive the second meaning, that is, desirous, because a thing that is in motion and wanders here and there seems to arouse in others a greater desire for it than one that stands still and which we can see at our ease. And since it seems inevitable that all those things we desire we should also love, and since, as we concluded earlier, it is not possible to love something that is not or does not seem to us beautiful, therefore, the word "charming" has acquired in everyday speech the meaning of beautiful, and "charm" the meaning of beauty. In this special sense, however, by which charm indicates that special beauty that has within it all those elements whereby anyone who looks upon it is obliged to become charmed (*vago*), that is, desirous; and having become desirous, his heart is always wandering to pursue it and enjoy it, his thoughts travel to her, and he becomes a vagabond in his mind.

Charm is, therefore, a beauty that attracts and sparks the desire to contemplate it and enjoy it. Thus we say "So-and-so is fairly charming" when we speak of a woman who has a certain sensual air and a certain desirability, mingled with virtue (*onestà*), and a certain attractiveness, such as Fiamminghetta has. Last night in a dream Venus told me that two years from now there will come, among the flowers of your Prato,[86] a woman from Pistoia whose name will be Lena and who will bring with herself the charm of her eyes. And even here among you there is one, whom I do not wish to name, who, in my judgment, is very attractive.

Mona Amorrorisca: You do well, lest any competition should arise between us and give occasion for scandal. But even if you do not name her, I see written on your face what you carry in your heart. But I will say nothing more, for to explain it is to ruin it.[87]

Celso: While others need three hints, you understand at the first. But let us now leave this and get back to our promises, according to which we still need to speak of loveliness (*venustà*).

Now note this. Cicero said there are two kinds of beauty, one of which consists in loveliness and the other in dignity, and that loveliness is appropriate to women, and dignity is appropriate to men. Therefore, according to this man, whose authority should be sufficient for you women, dignity is as important in a man as loveliness in a woman, since dignity in man is nothing other than an air of true nobility, full of reverence and admiration. Therefore, loveliness in a woman will be a noble air, chaste, virtuous, reverent, admiring, and, in her every movement, full of a modest loftiness, as Gualanda Forella can show you if you look at her free from all spite.

Those who have little knowledge (and are wont in their great presumption to disapprove of those who labor all day for knowledge) say that the word loveliness derives from the goddess of Love,[88] whom the poets know as the mother of sensual love, and thus logically indicates nothing else but beauty that is sensually beautiful. I think it is appropriate to say a little something in order to deliver you from this error, if you were in error, which I do not think is the case, and also those who, for this reason,[89] might disapprove of me—and they are many.

Now note. Two Venuses are described by the ancient writers. One, daughter of the Earth, operates in earthly and sensual ways, and the acts of physical love are supposed to originate from her. The other, they said, is the daughter of Heaven; her thoughts, deeds, manners, and words, are celestial, chaste, pure, and holy. And they claimed that from this second Venus comes loveliness, and those things that are lovely rather than sensual.[90]

Now we must speak of the air (*aria*), and here you must lend the ears

Raphael, *Joanna of Aragon* (Paris, Louvre; courtesy of Giraudon/Art Resource, NY). "*. . . loveliness in a woman will be a noble air, chaste, virtuous, reverent, admiring. . . .*"

Titian, *Sacred and Profane Love* (Rome, Galleria Borghese; courtesy of Alinari/Art Resource, NY). *"Two Venuses are described by the ancient writers. One, daughter of the Earth, operates in earthly and sensual ways. . . . The other, they said, is the daughter of Heaven . . . celestial, chaste, pure, and holy."*

of your intellect very carefully. My dear ladies, there is a proverb among the Latins (and the great authority of proverbs among the Ancients is easily seen by their frequency in the writings not only of the Latins but also of the Greeks), it is a proverb, then, that *conscientia, mille testes,* which means "a pure and clean conscience is worth a thousand witnesses." Assuming, therefore, this proverb to be very true, we will say that all those women who have stained their conscience with that foulness that defaces and sullies the purity and cleanness of the will, a foulness caused by the misuse of reason, for they are pierced all day long by the recollection of their fault and shaken by the evidence of the thousand witnesses of their wounded conscience, these women fall into a certain disease of the soul that continually worries and upsets them. This upset and worry produces such an arrangement of the humors that with their vapors they soil and stain the purity of the face and especially of the eyes which, as was said before, are the ministers and messengers of the heart. These vapors produce such an expression in the eyes, or, as is generally said, a certain bad air that indicates and reveals the infirmity of the soul not any differently than the paleness of the cheeks and of other features indicates the diseases and imbalances of the body and the upsets and agitations of its humors. Nor should it seem strange to you that a disease of the soul should upset the organs of the body, for experience illustrates every day how the pangs of the soul can cause a fever in the body and sometimes death.

Once you recognize this bad air as an indication and a revelation of the infection in the soul of the sick women I have mentioned, you will easily recognize the good air of those who are healthy, since as Aristotle says it well in the fifth book of his *Ethics,* that once we know one opposite, we cannot help but know the other opposite.[91] A little further down in the same book, he shows this much more clearly when he says: "If the good habits of the body are evident in the firmness and thickness of the flesh, the bad habits must then be evident in its flabbiness and thinness."[92]

Following this reasoning, you will clearly understand that when one says a woman "has an air about her" it means that this is a good sign, manifesting a clear, healthy soul and conscience, since by saying simply "air," by antonomasia[93] (which we perhaps would more properly call *par excellence*), we imply "good air." And a bad air, or not to have an air, implies a sign, a countenance, that reveals a disease of the heart and the ruins of a contaminated conscience.

Mona Amorrorisca: Your explanation of this passage has truly been beautiful and worthy of great consideration, both for being true and for being new, and certainly worthy of your intelligence much more than of our intellect. Nonetheless, since you have explained it for us so clearly, we have been quite capable of understanding it. But we will wait for another time to sing your praises fully and so, in silence, we wait to hear what you will say about majesty.

Celso: I don't know what else to say about majesty (*maestà*) except that it is a common expression in daily speech. When a woman is tall, well-shaped, carries herself well, sits with grandeur, speaks with gravity, laughs with modesty, and finally exudes the aura of a queen, then we say "That woman seems majestic; she has majesty." This expression is derived from the royal throne, where every act, every deed must be worthy of admiration and reverence. Thus majesty is nothing else but the movement and carriage of a lady who moves with a certain royal pomp, of a woman, I say, who is a somewhat tall and robust. And if you wish to see a certain example of this, look at the most illustrious lady, the Countess da Vernio, who with her royal presence, acts, manners, words, always shows to whomever does not otherwise know her that she is the sister of my most magnificent lord, Signor Gualterotto de' Bardi, and most acceptable consort of the most genteel and modest Signor Alberto, and, finally, that she is highborn and nobly married. And this is all I need tell you for now about beauty in general and all its related aspects, not that I think I have fully satisfied your desires.

Mona Lampiada: Since I am the oldest, I would not be considered presumptuous if I answer on behalf of everybody. And so I say that you have satisfied us much more than we would have dared to ask, even though from you one can expect great things. Nonetheless, we would like to have our understanding confirmed by the example of that chimera[94] you promised to create for us.

Celso: You are indeed very old, and you plainly show it, not with your face, which is as fresh and smooth as any other's (and I say this with all respect to all the ladies here, though you might no longer be in the flower of youth), but rather with your intellect, your intelligence, and your many other virtues about which it is better to be silent than to say little. You could not have said it better than to say Chimera, for just as the Chimera is imagined and cannot be found, so also that beautiful woman we wish to create will be imagined and not be found. And we will sooner see what one should have in order to be beautiful than what one has, without disparaging on account

Bronzino, *Lucrezia Panciatichi* (Florence, Uffizi; courtesy of Alinari/Art Resource, NY). *"When a woman is tall, well-shaped, carries herself well, sits with grandeur, speaks with gravity, laughs with modesty, and . . . exudes the aura of a queen, . . . she has majesty."*

of this the beauty of you ladies here present or of others who are not here. Although they themselves do not embody complete beauty, nevertheless, they have enough of it to be complimented and considered beautiful. Now let us come to our chimera.

No sooner had Celso opened his mouth to begin than the beautiful Gemmula from Pozzonuovo[95] appeared on the hill, all modesty, all gentility, and truly a precious pearl. Having heard about this gathering, she, like an intelligent woman, was drawn to the sound of these discussions. She had with her that clear diamond that, with the crown of many virtues, ennobles the square of San Francesco.[96] No sooner had they arrived on the hilltop than nearly all the other young ladies who were in the garden came to call them, singing, laughing, and, as is the custom in such parts, teasing, so much so that Celso was forced to abandon the undertaking and go with them to a beautiful repast prepared by Mona Simona de' Benintendi, a wise and venerable Florentine matron and wife of the owner of the garden.[97] She is such a fine lady that, in order to mention just some of her praises, it would be necessary to lengthen this dialogue with too many words. Once the snack was finished, they danced, sang, and did all those things that are appropriate to an honest company of noble and virtuous ladies and gentle and dear youths. And so they carried on until it was time for everyone to go home.

End of the First Dialogue

Second Dialogue

Because the young ladies who had been on the hilltop during the past discussion were left with a strong desire to see the form of that beautiful woman Celso had promised to paint for them, they begged Mona Lampiada to decree a place where, on another day, their wish could be fulfilled. And so Mona Lampiada, who had listened to Celso's words no less willingly than they, or at least had appeared to do so, had her husband, who was himself a bright man, invite Celso and these ladies to the next party at their house, together with other relatives of theirs, so as to pass an evening in honorable company. It was on this occasion that Celso, who had been duly entreated to continue, made a modest excuse and then went on to say:

Celso: It is evident that nature has been a free and generous bestower of her graces to mankind in general. The same, however, does not seem to be the case with individuals. In fact, daily experience leads us to affirm that nature has been very stingy and meager when it comes to individuals. As I said the last time, she did give everything, yes, but not to each person. As a matter of fact, she barely gave one thing to each person. To express this concept, the Ancients represented Nature as a woman full of breasts; mankind, unable to suck at more than one nipple at a time, can draw to himself only a small portion of her nutrition. Furthermore, if you consider carefully the nature of breasts, you will realize that in spite of the abundant nutrition they contain, as everyone knows, still they do not, on their own, pour their milk into the baby's mouth. The baby must suck the milk himself. This means nothing more than that, in many things, we must weary ourselves with art, industry, and wits in order to acquire or embellish or maintain them. And since the channel from which the milk flows is so small that barely a drop at a time comes out, we can infer that Nature does not bestow her graces generously but barely one thing to each person, one at a time. For this reason one finds few perfectly beautiful women. The one with a beautiful body does not have a delicate face, as is the case with Mona Altea from Three Canals. And there's the woman with a delicate face, but a short body, such as Mona Fiore from the Belltower. And the woman adorned with the most beautiful eyes, such as Mona Lucida from via de' Sarti, does not have a nice complexion. And so, in order to draw a woman who is, if not in everything at least for the most part, perfect, it is necessary, as I said at our other discussion, to take the best particular beautiful parts from all four of you and to create from them a woman as beautiful as we wish.

Before we deal with the body, however, I would first like us to prepare the colors. Not just white and black which, according to those who have written about it, are foremost, but all the colors we need, so that there will be no need afterward to interrupt our work. The colors we require, then, are blonde, tawny, black, red, fair,[1] white, vermillion, and flesh-pink.

You must know, then, that the color blonde is a yellow that is neither too bright nor too clear, but leaning more toward tan, with somewhat more luster. Even though it is not quite like gold, nonetheless, poets often compare it to gold. As you know, they often say, as Petrarch did in many places, that her hair is like fine gold.

Weaving a garland of thick, polished gold.[2]

Her golden hair was flowing in the breeze.[3]

You know that the proper and true color of hair should be blonde.[4]

There are two types of tawny: one tending toward yellow (and this is not for me) and another, called tan, tending toward a darker hue, and two brush-strokes of this will be enough for us.

Black does not need much of an explanation because everyone is familiar with it. That Florentine lady whom you welcomed so well takes very good advantage of it.[5] The darker and deeper this color is, the finer and more beautiful it is.

Red is that bright color we find in cochineal,[6] in corals, in rubies, the leaves of the pomegranate flower, and such things. Some reds are more or less intense, some more or less vivid, as we see in the objects I have mentioned.

Vermillion is almost a kind of red, but less vivid. In short, it resembles the cheeks of beautiful Francolina from via di Palazzuolo[7] when she is in a temper. I think this girl wins the prize for the brightest complexion in town. But let's leave that and return to the color vermillion, which we can find precisely in that wine we call *vermiglia* here in Tuscany.

Flesh-pink, also called *imbalconato,* is a white shaded with red, or a red shaded with white, such as the roses we call incarnate (*imbalconate*).[8] When these roses arrived in these parts, not so very long ago, they were so highly prized that whoever had one would put it in a beautiful little vase full of water, so that it would remain green and fresh longer, and then put it on the balcony, as a rare and novel thing, for the neighbors to see. And this is how that rose came to be called *imbalconata,* or "on the balcony."[9]

Because I spoke at length of the difference between white and fair in my other dialogue,[10] I need not repeat it now.

Having prepared the colors we need for the face, we can now begin with greater ease. The first part I would like us to draw is the hair, so that we do not forget it, as we did the last time.[11] The hair, then, according to what writers have said about it from time to time in their works, should be fine and blonde, sometimes similar to gold, sometimes to honey, sometimes like the bright rays of a clear sun, wavy, thick, abundant, long, as Apuleius, whom I mentioned before, said in the work I cited.[12] Speaking of its importance, its essence, of its every quality and detail, Apuleius says these very words which I will try to repeat in our language as they sound in Latin, which is impossible to do, yet I'll try. He says,

> If you will remove from the resplendent head of any beautiful young woman the splendor of the clear light of her blonde hair, you will see that head bereft of every beauty, despoiled of every grace, lacking every elegance. Even if she were that same Venus who was conceived in heaven, born of the sea, nurtured by the waves, surrounded by the Graces, and accompanied by her Amorini,[13] girt with the girdle of sensual desire, adorned with fascination, colored with charms, embellished with a thousand sweet and flattering enchantments, I say Venus, that beautiful Venus who, among the three fairest goddesses was judged to be the most beautiful and won the apple of beauty,[14] this goddess, deprived of the light, the splendor, the ornament of her golden hair, would be liked by no one, not even her beloved Vulcan, her husband and tender lover.[15] How wonderful it is to see an elegant woman with thick hair gathered in abundant locks upon her head, or falling in ample waves upon her shoulders![16]

According to what this worthy man tells us, the hair, then, is so important to the perfection of a beautiful woman and deserves so much care and honor that, besides what has already been said, Dion, a most illustrious Greek writer,[17] in his beautiful oration in praise of it, places among ignorant and worthless men those who do not take care of their hair with curlers, bodkins, and irons. And he points out that the Ancients, who slept on the ground, would keep their hair suspended on pieces of wood so

Titian, *Lady at Her Toilette* (Paris, Louvre; courtesy of Giraudon/Art Resource, NY). *"The hair . . . should be fine and blonde, sometimes similar to gold, sometimes to honey, sometimes like the bright rays of a clear sun, wavy, thick, abundant, long. . . ."*

as not to ruin it. This shows that the Ancients esteemed hair so highly that, for their sake, they thought little of the ease and rest of sweet sleep, the one and only true rest from all human toil. What more? The Spartans, raised under the severe laws of Lycurgus,[18] took such good care of their hair that, as we read, those three hundred men who fought so valiantly against

Darius, King of the Persians, which is all you read about in the ancient stories, while they waited for the bloody event, never neglected the care of their hair.[19] The great Homer gives as the chief ornament of the beauty of his Achilles the splendor of his thick hair.[20] And when Apuleius, whom I have already mentioned several times, discusses what makes hair beautiful, he adds these words:

> Such is the dignity of the hair that even though a very beautiful woman should bedeck herself very sumptuously with gold and pearls, and cover herself in very rich clothes, and should go out adorned in all the fashion and ornament that can be imagined, if she has not arranged her hair in a pleasing fashion and set it in a charming skillful way, one would never say that she was either beautiful or elegant.[21]

Since we have come to know how important hair is, and how it should be, we can see that Verdespina's hair has all the qualities we discussed, and so we will take hers for our ideal woman.

Selvaggia: Lena, bring the scissors here so we can cut it. But how would you like her to cut it? Close-cropped?

Celso: I do not want her to crop it off short, nor with scissors, but with the knife of imagination. Just see how Selvaggia makes fun of everything I say. And yet, she is wrong, because I am not teasing her. Oh well, patience! One day, perhaps, she will realize the error of her ways, but nothing else will help us now. But to get back to our discussion, now that we have fine blonde hair, tidy, wavy, abundant, long, lustrous, and well arranged, we must find the body on which to place it. We must not be like the man who was given some plants and, while he was looking for a garden in which to plant them, let them dry out and they died; and thus, because of the recipient's ineptitude the gift was thrown away.

Selvaggia: Well, then, Verdespina, you did well not to cut it off yet. Celso is so particular he might take too long to find the body on which to put your hair. He is not a man to be satisfied with the first thing, and in the meantime, perhaps, your hair would have spoiled.

Celso: No one here knows better than you whether I am too particular or too easily pleased. Nonetheless, I have given you the lie because I have already well found the right body, namely Mona Amorrorisca's. If my eyes, trusty appraisers of beauty, do not deceive me, she is close enough to the particular height we are looking for. One likes a robust body, with nimble, capable limbs, well placed and well proportioned. But I would not want my ideal beauty to be too big or very fat.

Selvaggia: Yet, even though Iblea Soporella is quite fat, she is still a very beautiful young lady who carries herself well, so upright, so nimble, so agile, so dexterous. Dear Lord! It is such a pleasure to see her move.

Celso: It is one of those things I have said a thousand times. These are graces that are bestowed upon a few people and not universally on every one. This young lady has such a majesty in her body, a beauty in her eyes, a grace in her face, a grandeur in her bearing, it seems her fatness has granted her that beauty, that agility which, in all other cases, it seems to take away. Not to mention her graciousness, her manner, her gentility and keen wit, and all those other gifts of the soul; I judge her to be one of the most beautiful women in these parts of town and I am sorry she is not here with us today.

Mona Lampiada: I had sent for her, but because of her father's death and her husband's illness she finds herself in the difficulties you know of, and does not believe it proper for her to come to a party. I am very disappointed about this, for she does cheer up everything.

Celso: Now, to go back to the body, I say that you, Mona Amorrorisca, have one that is somewhere between lean and fat, plump and juicy, of the right proportions, one in which we find agility and dexterity, together with a certain something that suggests the aura of a queen. Its color is not the white that slides into pallor, but that white, tinged with blood, that was so prized by the Ancients. The body of a gentlewoman must move with gravity and in a certain genteel way so as to carry her uprightly, yet not stiffly, giving her that majesty we mentioned earlier. Because you have the majority of these qualities, we must put Verdespina's hair on you. And so we will go on to look for a forehead.

The forehead must be broad, that is, wide, high, fair, and serene. Many people prefer the height, which is measured from the hairline to the edge of the eyebrows and the nose, to be a third of the face; the second third is down to the upper lip, and the last third all the rest including the entire chin. The height, then, must be half its width; and so the forehead must be twice as wide as it is high, since the length is measured from the height and

Titian, *La Bella* (Florence, Pitti; courtesy of Alinari/Art Resource, NY). *"The body . . . is somewhere between lean and fat, plump and juicy, of the right proportions, one in which we find agility and dexterity, together with a something that suggests the aura of a queen."*

the height from the length. I said fair because it should not be a washed-out white, without any luster, but shiny like a mirror; not shiny because of lotions or polishes or powders, like those of Bovinetta del Maleficio,[22] who, if she were fish for frying, would cost more than a penny a pound because it would not need to be floured; but she is neither for sale nor for frying.[23]

The line of the brow must not be absolutely flat, but curved, like a bow, so gently that it is hardly noticeable. From the turn of the temples, however, it must descend more quickly. Our poets call such a forehead serene, and rightly so, because, just as the clear sky that has no trace of cloud or any manner of spot is called serene, so the forehead that is clear, open, without furrows or spots, without powders, quiet, and tranquil, can right-fully be called serene. And just as when the sky is serene it engenders a certain contentment in the soul of he who looks upon it, so, too, the forehead we call serene through the eyes pleases the soul of those who gaze upon it. This happens to me, when I look upon Mona Lampiada's forehead which, having all the qualities I have listed, will be fit to be placed under Verdespina's hair.

The serenity I have just described is much increased by the luster of the eyes which, though they are outside the bounds of the forehead, nonethe-less seem to be like the two great luminaries in the sky. Beginning with the eyebrows, we must now speak of the eyes, and we will take our example from Verdespina, who has eyebrows the color of ebony, thin, with short, soft hairs, as if they were of fine silk. They grow gently thinner from their middle to their extremities, on one side up to the hollow or socket of the eye, toward the nose, and on the other toward that part which is near the ear, and there they end.

Next come the eyes, which in their rounded part, that is in the eyeball, must be, except for the pupil, white in color, leaning a little toward flax, but so little it is hardly noticeable. The pupils, then, except for that little circle in the middle, should not be perfectly black, even though all the Greek and Latin poets, and ours as well, unanimously praise black eyes, and they all agree the goddess of beauty had them like that. Nevertheless, there is no scarcity of those who praise blue eyes that tend toward the color of the sky, and it is written by very trustworthy authors that beautiful Venus had them like that. Among you there is a woman reputed to be very beautiful by me and many others, who has them like that and seems to gain grace from them. Nevertheless, common usage seems to have established that dark tan is, among all colors, the foremost color for the eyes. Blackberry black is not

Bronzino, *Eleonora of Toledo de' Medici with Giovanni de' Medici* (Florence, Uffizi; courtesy of Alinari/Art Resource, NY). *". . . the eyes . . . must be, except for the pupil, white in color, leaning a little toward flax. . . ."*

much to be praised because it produces a somewhat dark and harsh gaze. Tan, that is, a dark tan, produces a sweet gaze, happy, clear, mild; and it gives to the movement of the eyes an undefinable alluring grace, honest and piercing, which now I do not want to explain in any other way save to show you those of Mona Lampiada, which lack none of these elements.

Besides those qualities already mentioned, eyes must be, like Mona Lampiada's, large and full, neither concave nor hollow, for hollowness makes for a proud gaze, whereas fullness makes for a beautiful and modest gaze. Wanting to praise Juno's eyes, Homer said they were like those of an ox, meaning they were round, full, and large.[24] Many have said they should be a little on the long side, others oval, which I do not mind.

Eyelids, when they are white and tinged with certain rosy little veins, hardly visible, help very much the general beauty of the eyes. Eyelashes must be thin, not very long, not white, since, besides creating a deformity, they impair the sight. Nor do I like them very black, for they would make for a frightened gaze.

The hollow which surrounds the eye should not be very deep, nor too wide, nor of a color different from the cheeks. Women should be careful, therefore, when they use cosmetics (those that have a darker complexion, I mean), because very often that part is badly suited to receiving color—or, to speak more clearly, eyeshadow—in its hollowness, or to keep it, because the motion of the eyelashes creates lines that look very bad. Mona Teofila's neighbor often falls into this error.

The ears, which painters depict more in the color of pale balas rubies than in ruby-red, in fact more like incarnate roses than red roses, I will take from you, Selvaggia. For them to be beautiful, as yours well show, it is necessary for them to be of a medium size, with the folds gracefully arranged and suitably raised, but of a brighter color than the flat parts. And the border that goes all around them must be transparent and resplendent with red, like the seeds of a pomegranate. What, above all, takes their grace away is their being limp and languid, just like their being firm and well set gives them grace.

There is not much to say about the temples, except that it is necessary that they be white and flat, not hollow, nor excessively raised, nor moist, nor so narrow that they seem to press on the brain, which would suggest a weak intellect. They are all the more beautiful the more they resemble those of Mona Amorrorisca, and the more the art of wearing the hair over them, or higher up, or lower down, or more wavy, or more smoothly, or thicker, or thinner, enlarges or diminishes them, makes them wider or narrower, longer or shorter, as is necessary, or when a pretty little flower adorns them.

Mona Lampiada: When I was a girl we did not put flowers in our hair, as our girls do nowadays. With so many flowers and leaves in their hair they often look like a pot of cloves or oregano. And there are some who look like a quarter kid on the spit, for they even wear rosemary. To me it seems the most graceless thing in the world. And what do you think of this, Messer Celso?

Celso: Not very much, to tell you the truth. Their mistake arises from their not knowing why, in the old days, the custom of wearing flowers in one's hair developed. I am speaking of gentlewomen, of course, because country-girls, who have neither gold nor pearls, fill their hair with flowers, as you know, without any order, style or measure, and in them this nonchalance is beautiful.

Mona Lampiada: I think even gentlewomen started to wear flowers in their hair around the house, instead of pearls or gold, since not all our peers had the means to adorn themselves with stones from the Orient or sand from the Tagus.[25] And so it became necessary to gather treasures from the gardens of our own land. But then everyone began to overdo it, so much so that sometimes it seems they have a garland around their face, or a Quintain.[26] Waters and powders were invented in order to remove scales, or freckles and other such marks, and today they are used to paint and to whiten the face, not unlike plaster or gypsum on the surface of walls. And perhaps these little simpletons believe that the men they seek to please are not aware of such concoctions which, besides ruining their skin and making them grow old before their time, also ruin their teeth and make them look like carnival clowns all year round. Think for a moment about Mona Betola Gagliana, what does she look like? The more she smooths her skin out, the more she makes herself up, the older she looks. She looks like a gold ducat that has been dropped in acid. She would not have turned out like that if, when she was younger, she had not groomed herself so much. For my part, if I have kept myself well (I do not know this, but it is enough that others say it), it is for no other reason than the well water that has always been my wash, and will be so for my little daughter as well, as long as she lives in my house, and after that her husband can worry about her.

But do tell us the reason for wearing flowers, for surely I have wandered a little far from home. But let the righteous indignation I feel toward these plastered-on faces be my excuse.

Celso: As you know, people generally sleep more on their right side than on their left. As a result, the right side, because it is more pressed down and crushed, becomes a little more flattened than the other side, as is evident even in men's beards which, for the same reason, are always thinner on the right than on the left. Now, because it was necessary to raise the flattened part, gentlewomen skillfully used to put a few flowers on it, some fine little flowers that would make it stand out a little, but not overshadow the other side. There were two kinds of flowers, both of the same color, a color that would enhance rather than overshadow the freshness of their vermillion cheeks and the fairness of the entire face, and that was azure blue. And so they picked cabbage flowers (*cappucci*)[27] and bluebonnets (*fioralisi*) which, because of this, came to be known among us by such names as "bonnet flowers" and "face flowers."[28] And this because, as you must have heard tell, in the old days women used to wear on their heads certain head-dresses they called bonnets; and because those flowers were placed under these bonnets they were called bonnet flowers, or flowers for bonnets, and they were used precisely to cover up the flattened temple I mentioned before. Bluebonnets, because they have a longer stem and can reach out toward the face, were called *fioralisi,* as if to say "flowers for the face" (*fior da visi*), or flowers appropriate for decorating the face. They also used sweet violets, for the short time they lasted, which in color and size somewhat resembled the other flowers. And they called them *viole mammole* as if to say violets for young girls (*mammole*), and for this reason Politian called them virginal little violets (*mammolette verginelle*), as if he wished to imply they were flowers, that is, violets, to decorate young virgins.[29]

Those violets many call clove-pinks[30] because of their fragrance, roses, and other such larger, more strongly smelling flowers were carried in the hand in those days. And so that their far-too-bright colors would not blanch the natural color of a rosy face, the women did not place them near their cheeks, for you know how the color red is usually inimical to your beautiful cheeks and your entire complexion. It would surprise me to find a lady who wore such flowers, were it not that I see everything is done by chance and that the art of attiring, dressing, and adorning oneself has been lost. What a clumsy thing it is to see a pair of fur cuffs on a fine Lucchese gown with open trimmings! Do they not realize that the fur trim puffs out the cuffs, and that the open trimmings disappear, and that the arm itself appears crippled? What a fine thing it is to see the neckline (*imbusto*) without a collar, or without a lining, but quite plain instead! So now, do arms get cold only from the elbow down and that's why we line the bottom half, but not the rest of the sleeve? What great foolishness! How very clumsy! How boorish! And still it is the custom, and we see it done by persons who think sweet orange blossoms stink.[31]

But, please, let us return to our flowers. And so I say that some Lady

Botticelli, "Flora," detail from *Primavera* (Florence, Uffizi; courtesy of Alinari/Art Resource, NY). *". . . flowers . . . would enhance . . . the freshness of their vermillion cheeks and the fairness of the entire face. . . ."*

Simpletons[32] came along who, without thinking too carefully about the matter, saw that one of those little flowers added so much charm, like Sophists,[33] philosophized in this manner: "If a little flower produces so much charm, what will a big flower do? And if one or two flowers do so much, what will ten or twelve, or an entire bunch of flowers do?" And they began to pour them on, as you see, without stopping to think whether the head was large, or the face long, or if the temples were hollow or full. If Panfilo's wife were a woman after my own heart, perhaps she would wear fewer flowers. Because her temples are a little set back, the gilly-flowers she places by her cheeks (as if she did not put any further down!) not only drain all the color from her face (as if she had any color to spare), but fill out her temples more than is necessary and so suggest that they are more hollowed than, in fact, is the case. Look at her carefully next time you meet her and you will see if I am telling you the truth or I know what I am talking about.

The cheeks require no further description because we have the perfect example in front of us: your cheeks, Selvaggia, which, even though they have gained some color at my words and now have an excess of what they did not lack before, I will now take for my picture of beauty. Nevertheless, in order to observe the order I have begun and to say more about them, I will say that the cheeks yearn for a more subdued fairness than the forehead, that is, a little less lustrous. At their sides their whiteness is as pure as snow. Then, as the cheeks swell they become fleshy-pink until, on their summit, they deepen into that reddish hue the sun leaves behind itself when it departs from our hemisphere in fine weather, and you know is nothing else but fairness shaded with vermillion.

We are left with choosing the nose, which is the most important element on the face of either a man or a woman for, as I said to you the other day, it is impossible for a woman without a totally perfect nose to appear beautiful in profile.[34] Sarto de' Cavagli's wife, who has a certain beauty from the front, looks like a witch in profile. I discovered this defect of hers one morning at Mass in the Chapel when she was standing in front of Selvaggia.[35] But let us return to the nose, whose proportions I discussed the other day and I need not repeat now. If anyone has forgotten, or was not there, just look at Verdespina's nose and you will remember. Like a second Juno, she has a most perfect nose.[36] Besides having the correct proportions, the nose (to follow the order we established) should tend toward the small and narrow from its base, which is above the mouth, to its tip. At the base there should be a slight curve, distinguished by a hint of color, but not red, with almost invisible creases that outline the two nostrils. These must first swell a little, then, sloping gently, rise to the tip as if drawn with the same curve. If, at the bridge of the nose, where the cartilage ends and the solid part begins there were a very little rise, not something aquiline, which usually is not pleasing in a woman, something akin to the joint of a finger, it would give the nose grace. In fact, it would be its very perfection.

The lower part, that is, all the cartilage, and especially its border, should be the same color as the ears, but perhaps even less bright, so long as it is not white-white, as if it were cold. The nostrils should be clean and dry. Many women have them somewhat moist, especially near the cheeks, and sometimes this gives a certain unpleasant impression. The ancient Latins had a proverb for this to indicate a man of good judgement: "*Est homo emunctis naribus,*" that is to say, "he is a man with a dry nose."[37]

A turned-up nose is not beautiful since, besides indicating a person overly disposed to be temperamental, it also spoils the profile, as can be seen with the wife of that certain teacher of ours who has a student in Pistoia,[38] who is otherwise a very beautiful young woman. The nose that is always about to fall into the mouth is also ugly.[39] But that nose that is evenly set on its base is pleasing, like yours, Verdespina, full of every grace and beauty.

Now we come to the mouth, source of all loving delights. It is desirable that it should tend toward small rather than large, nor should it be pointed or flat. And when it opens, especially when it opens either to laugh or to speak, it should not show more than five, or at most six, upper teeth. The lips should not be too thin, nor overly thick, but such that their vermillion may show against the flesh-pink that surrounds them. When the mouth closes they must meet equally, so that the upper lip does not extend further than the lower, nor the lower further than the upper. And at their inside edge they must grow smaller so as to form an obtuse angle, such as this one

and not an acute angle

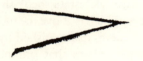

nor like the chin.

It is quite true that, when the lower lip swells a little more in the middle than the upper lip, with a little mark that nearly seems to divide it into two parts, that that little swelling, especially if the mouth is open, gives much grace to the entire mouth. Between the upper lip and what you call the tip of the nose there ought also to appear a little space that looks like a little furrow, slightly indented, sown with flesh-pink roses.

Occasionally, closing the mouth with a sweet movement or with a certain grace on the right side, in order to open it on the left, as if with a hidden smile, or sometimes biting the lower lip in an unaffected way, nonchalantly, so that these gestures do not seem to be simperings or affectations, but are done rarely, modestly, sweetly, with a little modest sensuousness, with a certain movement of the eyes which, at one moment, gaze steadily ahead, and then, suddenly, look down, which is a pretty thing, these are gestures which open, which throw wide open a paradise of delights and flood with an incomprehensible sweetness the heart of the man who gazes at them with yearning.

But all of this would amount to nothing if the beauty of the teeth did not concur by being small, but not minuscule, square, equal, separated in an orderly fashion, fair, and, above all, like ivory. They should be bordered, tied, and sustained by the gums, which should appear to be borders of scarlet satin rather than of red velvet. And if by chance it should happen that the tip of the tongue should be seen, and this should be rarely, this will add charm, yearning, and consolation if it will be brazil-wood red,[40] small, but neither pointed nor square. And Mona Lampiada has an overall graceful mouth, such as I would like it; Selvaggia the lips, which are marvelous; Mona Amorrorisca the teeth, and Verdespina the gums and tongue, so that with all four of you we will make one of the most beautiful mouths that ever was, not just painted in a picture, but even imagined. For this reason each of you will give me her share for my chimera's portrait.

From you, Verdespina, I will take the chin. Among all of you ladies, all of whom have beautiful chins, Verdespina seems to me to have the most beautiful because it is not curved up, nor pointed, but is round and colored in a light vermillion, a little brighter on its rise. From the lower lip where it ends, to the jaw, where it begins, it has a certain sweetness that can better be considered with the mind than expressed in words. And from its base, rising halfway up toward the lip, it should lose color rather than not, for it will regain it as it continues its pleasant voyage toward the lip. A small dimple in the place I mentioned in the last discussion is its own particular sign of beauty.[41] Vallera showed that he was well aware of this when, praising the beauties of his beloved, he said:

> My Nencia has a hole in her chin
> that makes her entire face more beautiful.[42]

There you have it, even farmers, full of natural good judgment, understand perfect beauty. If the chin I have described should then slope toward the throat and run into a slight rise, it gains in overall beauty. And in fat women it is the foremost ornament, and a sweet companion to the beauties of the throat.

The throat must be round, slender, fair, and without a spot. As it turns here or there, it must make folds that show now one, now the other of the two chords on either side of the vital veins,[43] with a beauty that is sweet to contemplate but difficult to describe. When it bends down it should make certain circular wrinkles around it in the shape of necklaces. When it bends up it should stretch completely as if to imitate the sensuous little stock-dove with its neck tinged in gold and purple. One likes a throat with very delicate skin, slender, long rather than short. At its border with the bosom it should reveal a little declivity, all filled with snow.[44] Above it, close to the chin-strap,[45] there should be a small swelling, but not such that, as in the case of men, it looks like the supposed apple of that ill-advised Adam.[46] Since I have gone along describing the throat by taking that of beautiful Selvaggia as an example, you should not be surprised that, for some time now, I have gazed so intently upon her. We will then take hers, perhaps the most beautiful throat that I have ever seen, and we will add it to our drawing, and it will supplement with its presence what I have not been able to draw with the rough paintbrush of my words.

Descending from the throat to the shoulders, we will say that when they have a certain form, such as yours, Mona Amorrorisca, very sweet and large (for narrowness offends the shoulders), they are truly perfect.

Let the neck be white, yet a little rosy. And if they are not equally flat, at least let the shoulders not swell so much that they seem to be have a hump.

And that quasi-valley that runs down from the nape of the neck to the loins should not be very deep because, on account of its own deformity, it would make the shoulders seem too big and the bodice too pronounced. When this happens, it looks ugly. And because these parts are very beautiful in Selvaggia and in Mona Amorrorisca, we will take the neck from Selvaggia, and from you we will take the shoulders. Coming back to consider the shoulders, we will say that as the shoulders progress from the base of the throat into the arms, they should rise a little, in the manner of handles from an ancient vase crafted by a master. Then, falling not too quickly, they should secure the arms and half restrain the neckline of the garments, so that they do not fall. And in this part, too, Mona Amorrorisca is quite distinguished.

Selvaggia: Well, my dear Messer Celso, show us how you form the shoulders and then the arms in the manner of an ancient vase. Preachers offer us poor little women examples in order to make us better understand their arguments, for this is necessary when dealing with coarse minds.[47]

Celso: I would be coarse if I held you ladies to have coarse minds and thought I could refine them. You ladies make us men look more coarse-minded than we would like. But if you would nevertheless like an example, what more beautiful or true example do you seek than that offered to us by Mona Lampiada? She is not just a vase, but certainly an entire treasure chest of all the virtues that adorn the spirit (*animo*)[48] of a gentlewoman. But since you could say to me that you want an ancient vase, not a modern one like hers, I will satisfy you.[49]

You see that the handles start by rising a little, and then they gently descend, as arms ought to. Since we have started drawing, I want to show you on an ancient vase how the throat rises from the conjunction of the bosom, the neck, and the shoulders, and how the bodice rises up from the waist. I do not think this will displease you. On the contrary, it will seem to you that either Nature has imitated Art, or that the art of your feminine beauty has drawn those beautiful vases. But first I want to get the beauty of the bosom out of the way.

The bosom must be, above all, white. Why waste more time? The bosom must be like Selvaggia's. Look at hers and you will see every perfection, all the correct proportions, every grace, every charm, every elegance, in short, every beauty. Here are violets in every season, roses in January, snow in August; here are the Graces, Loves, enticements, flatteries, adulations; here is Venus with all her court, with all the heavenly gifts, her girdle, her veil, her tresses, her ribbons, in short, in all her splendor. Not only is there nothing lacking, but here is more than desire can hope for, more than the intellect can understand, than memory remember, than the tongue express, than imagination fathom; so much so that there is no need to waste any more words. I, for one, believe neither Helen, nor Venus, nor the goddess of beauty had a more beautiful or more admirable bosom.[50]

Selvaggia: Oh, go on, go on! Tell us how it should be formed, as you have done with all the other parts. I would not want you, by either feigning to do me such a favor or by teasing me, to forego the description of one of the most important parts, in my humble opinion, that one finds in a beautiful woman.

Celso: You will have to excuse me; I do not have it in me to say anything that would not be a far cry from that most beautiful and most fortunate exemplar of yours.

Selvaggia: Granting that you speak the truth, nonetheless, I beg you to describe its beauty, if only for my sake, since I cannot see my own bosom.

Celso: If only you would let others see it! Well then, since I am your prisoner, I must do as you please. Nevertheless, I will deal with it quickly because of what has just been said and because, in the other dialogue, I said almost enough about it. We will say, then, that a beautiful bosom, besides having breadth, its chief ornament, is also so plump that no sign of bones can be seen. Rising softly from the sides, it swells in such a way as to be hardly noticeable by the eye. It should be a very fair color tinged with roses. In this bosom the fresh and lively breasts, heaving as though ill at ease at being constantly oppressed and confined by the garments, showing they want to escape from their prison, rise up so resolutely and vigorously that they force the viewer's eyes to rest firmly upon them, and thereby thwart their escape. You ladies say they must be well set, and you like those that are small, but not, as one of your friends, Mona Selvaggia, said, that they look like the rosettes on the lyre King David carried in the play at San Felice in Piazza.[51]

Now then, having said this to satisfy Selvaggia, even though she has never satisfied me with a single glance, I will show you, as I promised, how an ancient vase illustrates the manner in which the body is formed, that is, how the bodice rises up from the waist, and the throat up from the bosom and the shoulders. Now examine these:

Do you see how the neck of that first vase rises up from the shoulders, and how much gracefulness the slenderness of the neck gives back to the body of the vase in return for what it receives, and how the curvature makes it stand out, beautiful and graceful? Consider now the second vase and look at how the neck rises from the body. It is a woman's bosom rising up from the waist; and the more the hips protrude, the more the bosom will seem slender and gentle, and require very little by way of a belt, as we see in the relationship of the shoulders to the throat evident in the first vase. This does not occur in the third vase where, as you may well see, there is neither gracefulness nor beauty.

Those women with a long and slender throat, and with wide, graceful shoulders, are similar to the first vase. Those with wide hips, the foremost attraction of shapely naked women, and of a gentle bosom, slender, well

Parmigianino, *Madonna of the Long Neck* (Florence, Pitti; courtesy of Alinari/Art Resource, NY). "*. . . how much gracefulness the slenderness of the neck gives back to the body . . . in return for what it receives. . . .*"

proportioned, are similar to the second vase. Certain poor gleaners,[52] without shape or charm, are similar to the third vase. And those women who were made without stint of material and were left unfinished, roughed out and sculpted with a hatchet, not with file and chisel, are similar to the fourth vase.

With this demonstration and with this example you will realize that the hips should be quite pronounced and should let the bosom rise from them, straightforward and elegant. And the shoulders must do the same for the throat. And though these parts can be helped with wadding and padding and, in a word, by the tailor's art, nonetheless, when Art is not helped by Nature she can do little, and the little she does do comes out badly, and only a few people do not notice it. It is like trying to look tall by wearing platform shoes, as everyone knows, except for the husband when he goes to bed at night.[53] And so, in conclusion, we will say that Nature is the mistress (*maestra*) of beauty, and Art is one of her handmaidens, and for our design we will take Mona Amorrorisca's pronounced hips, and from them we will go down to the legs.

Selvaggia will give us her legs, long, thin, and straightforward in their lower part; but with calves as large as they need be, as white as snow and as rounded as necessary; with shins not so devoid of flesh that the shinbones can be seen, but comfortably full, so that the leg is not overly thick. The heels will not be too pronounced, nor so flat that they will not be noticed.[54]

We like small feet, slender, but not thin, springing neatly from the ankle. Homer said Thetis's were silvery.[55] I say they should be as white as alabaster when they are to be seen bare. I would be happy to see them covered with thin, narrow, close-fitting shoes, cut with true skill. A finely crafted shoe for long feet will have cross-cuts, for wide feet the cuts will be length-wise but short, proportioned, appropriate, imaginative, and always in a new style. Be sure slippers are short, low, and tidy. But what am I doing, usurping the office of Mona Raffaella from the Academy of the Intronati![56] And you, Selvaggia, will give me your most slender feet for our chimera.

Now that we have shown you the perfection of a beautiful woman by pointing out examples of beauty in all four of you ladies, I would like to give her, so as to finish her better, grace and elegance and all those other elements appropriate to the complete perfection of consummate beauty, as we described them to you the other day. Then we will put an end to this for it is about time. But tell me the truth, do you not think this picture I have drawn in your minds has come out more beautiful, using the four of you, than that famous "Helen" Zeuxis created from the five women of Croton?[57] This is very strong proof that today, in Prato, women are much more beautiful than they were in ancient Greece.[58]

Verdespina: How can that be? Why, your perfect woman has neither arms nor hands, so just imagine how she is! Why, that statue at the bottom of the stairs down at the Court of Justice is more beautiful than yours; though she, too, has no arms, at least she has a hinge that lets her hold an iron mace in her hands.[59]

Celso: You are quite right, young lady. Poor me, what have I done? Just look at what I had forgotten! This is because of Selvaggia, who always leads me astray. Had she been satisfied with letting her bosom serve for our picture without further descriptions, I would not have made this mistake because just then I wanted to proceed to talk about the part that Verdespina has called me back to.

Selvaggia: Little by little, according to this man, I am the root of all evil. I will soon start to believe you dislike me.

At this point a certain old woman who had come to accompany one, I do not know which, of these women home, all of a sudden said: "Oh, what are you saying, my young girl! Why, don't you realize he's teasing you, you silly girl? If only my master liked me as much, I wouldn't have to suffer through an entire winter with only one pair of clogs."[60]

As everyone burst into laughter, the old woman stood up and went into the kitchen. Then Celso, when everyone had stopped laughing, continued saying: "Selvaggia, I cannot deny what the old woman said is true, but . . .

Selvaggia: Here is that "but" that ruins everything. But in the name of God, even though I am not such a beauty that one cannot find something to criticize about me, at least I am not like this beauty of yours that has taken you two days to create and has neither arms nor hands. Oh, she came out well, the pretty thing! I, at least, have them, but or no but.

Celso: You will not have them for long, if you are going to be angry, because for the sake of that love I will take them from you and place them on my creation. And if she had nothing more than your bosom and all the other things she has from you, she would still be beautiful, whether you like it or not. We will then take your arms because they are of that well-proportioned length we showed you the other day in the squaring of the human figure.[61] On top of this, they are very white, with a slight shade of flesh-pink on the raised parts, fleshy and muscular, but with a certain softness so that they seem to be not Hercules' arms when he squeezed Cacus,[62] but Pallas's arms when she stood before the shepherd.[63] They must be full of a natural substance that gives them a certain vigor and freshness which in turn generates such a firmness that, if you press it with a finger, the flesh will give way under the finger and immediately turn white, but the moment the finger is raised the flesh rises again and the whiteness disappears and lets the flesh-pink color return.

The hands, which everyone agrees are most beautiful in you (I am speaking to you, Selvaggia, and it will do you no good to cover them), also ought to be white, especially on the upper side; large and somewhat full, the palm a little hollow and shadowed with roses. The lines must be clear and quite distinct, well marked, not tangled nor crossed. The mounds of Jupiter, Venus, and Mercury must be quite distinct, but not too high.[64] The line of the intellect must be deep and clear and not crossed by any other line. That hollow between the index finger and the thumb should be well set, without wrinkles, and of a lively color. Fingers are beautiful when they are long, straight, delicate, and slightly tapering toward the end, but so little as to be scarcely perceptible. Fingernails should be clear and like balas rubies tied with flesh-pink roses and pomegranate leaves; not long, not round, nor completely square, but with a fine shape and a very slight curve; bare, clean, well kept, so that that little white crescent at their base is always visible. At the top the nail should extend past the flesh of the finger the thickness of a small knife, without the least suspicion of a black rim at the tip.[65] The hand as a whole ought to be delicately soft, as if we were touching fine silk or the softest cotton. And this is what we wanted to say about the arms and the hands. Now my creation will not be like that statue in the square. The thought of comparing it to that! You really are like one of those sharp thorns that get in between the flesh and the nail, and green, so that it goes in better.[66]

Selvaggia: Now I believe your picture is like one of those wrought by the hands of a good master. To tell you the truth, it has come out very beautiful, so much so that if I were as much of a man as I am a woman, I would have to fall in love with it, like a new Pygmalion.[67] And do not think that I say she is beautiful because of those parts we ladies have given her, but rather because of the adornments you have bestowed upon her, and the guise under which you have presented her in your description is such that it would make Iacopo Cavallaccio's wife appear beautiful. Speaking only for myself, I for one, if I had as beautiful a bosom as you have preached in your well-chosen words, would not yield to Helen, nor Venus, nor Beauty herself.

Celso: You have it, and you know it. It is not necessary at this time to carry on like this. Good for you and for the man who is worthy enough to look upon it sometime. And truly, when that friend of mine composed that beautiful elegy in praise of it, having had such a fine occasion for it, it is not surprising he painted such a beautiful canvas.[68]

But in order to give our chimera her final perfection, and so that she should not lack anything to be desired in a beautiful woman, you, Mona Lampiada, will give her that loveliness that sparkles in your eyes, that fine air which emanates from the well-proportioned union of your members. You, Mona Amorrorisca, will give her the regal majesty of your person, the cheerfulness of your honest and respectable appearance, the deliberate gait and the dignified manner of resting your eyes on something, in that gracious manner that so delights anyone who beholds it. A composed elegance, an appetizing charm, an attraction that is honest, sensuous, severe, sweet will come from Selvaggia, with her compassionate cruelty, which one is obliged to praise, though one does not desire it.[69] You, Verdespina, will give her the grace that so endears you, the readiness and sweetness of cheerful, witty, honest, and elegant speech. Intelligence and the other gifts and virtues of the soul are not our business because I have tried to paint the beauty of the body, not that of the soul. For the latter, a better painter than I is needed, with better colors and better brushes than those of my feeble abilities, even though your example is no less sufficient in this beauty than in the other.

And without saying anything more, they ended their discussion and everyone went home.

Notes

Proem

1. The Italian original reads "Mona Ciona" and "Mona Bettola." In this context Ciona is probably used as a diminutive of Sempliciona (simpleton), while Bettola is another word for a tavern.

2. The woman in black satin is Mona Ciona, mentioned below.

3. In this translation we retain the title *Mona,* used to indicate a married woman (Mrs.), as in Leonardo da Vinci's painting *Mona Lisa* (Lisa, wife of Francesco Giocondo).

4. Firenzuola is using fairly plebian names, as if to say Lady This or Lady That.

5. Clement VII (Giulio de' Medici, 1478–1534), pope from 1523. Giulio, the orphaned illegitimate son of Giuliano de' Medici, was raised in Florence in the household of his uncle, Lorenzo the Magnificent, where he received a humanist education. His ecclesiastical career began under the sponsorship of his cousin Giovanni (1475–1521), who later became Pope Leo X (1513). Clement was a patron of arts and letters, gathering around him such eminent figures as Raphael, Michelangelo, and Cellini, and founding the Laurenziana Library in Florence. The literary circle that gathered around his papal court at Rome included such famous humanists as Cardinal Pietro Bembo, Bishop Paolo Giovio, and the writer Annibal Caro. In 1526 Clement VII dispensed Firenzuola of his monastic vows.

6. Firenzuola is referring to *The Expulsion of the New Letters Unnecessarily Added to the Tuscan Language* (*Discacciamento delle nuove lettere inutilmente aggiunte nella lingua toscana*), a treatise in which he argues against the proposed introduction of several Greek letters into the Italian alphabet.

7. This is the *Discourses on Love* (*Ragionamenti d'amore*). In 1525 Firenzuola dedicated the "First Day" of this as yet unfinished collection to the Duchess Maria Caterina Cibo. The work was intended to be a collection of thirty-six short stories narrated over the course of six days by a company of elegant young people, in this case three men and three ladies. Firenzuola, however, completed only the six tales for the "First Day" and a few more tales for the other "Days." The incomplete collection was published posthumously in the *Prose di M. Agnolo Firenzuola* (Florence, 1552).

8. To bear witness to his moment of glory at the papal court, Firenzuola calls upon, quite appropriately, the best-known historian in contemporary Rome, Paolo Giovio (1483–1552), named Bishop of Nocera in 1528. Giovio, one of the great intellectual lights at the courts of the two Medici popes, Leo X and Clement VII, is

best known for his *Historiarum sui temporis,* which covers the period 1494–1547, and his *Elogia,* a series of biographical sketches.

9. Marcus Tullius Cicero (106–43 BCE), Roman orator and writer famous for his *Orations* and *Letters.* His public life, dedicated to the defense of Roman republican ideals, became a model for civic virtue. His elegant Latin prose style was much admired and emulated by Renaissance humanists, to the point that some extremists argued against the use of Latin words, expressions, or constructions not found in Cicero's writings.

10. Lucius Lucceius, a praetor and friend of Cicero, was very active in Roman politics. During the 50s BCE Lucceius wrote a history of Rome covering the years 90–81 BCE.

11. This is Firenzuola's fanciful creation from a comment made in the most prosaic if impatient terms by Cicero to Atticus, to the effect that he had asked Lucceius to write his biography. See Cicero's *Letters to Atticus* IV, 6.

12. In this case Helen may be representative of earthly or mortal beauty, Venus of heavenly or divine beauty.

13. This comment, voiced not by Celso but by the narrator himself, is directed at the historical woman who served as a model for Selvaggia.

14. We have no historical record of any Mona Biurra who lived near the "picture" (that is, near a roadside shrine with a picture, probably of the Virgin Mary), as her nickname "dalla Immagine" seems to suggest.

15. See below, pp. 16–17, for Celso's summary of Aristophanes' creation myth from Plato's *Symposium.* Firenzuola may have been left physically scarred by syphilis.

16. The Fates were thought to have both beneficial and harmful powers over human beings. Firenzuola is suggesting that, in his case, the Fates have ruined, not improved, his lot in life. This again may be an oblique reference to the ravages of syphilis which Firenzuola suffered.

17. Firenzuola is trying to be amusing by blaming his wet nurse for the present size of his nose.

18. Ital.: *bandito la croce addosso* (banished wearing the cross). A reference to heretics who were banished or kept in isolation and forced to wear a habit marked with a cross. See, for example, the description of Menocchio's house arrest in the village of Montereale and the obligation to "wear over his clothing the *habitello* with the painted cross, the sign of his infamy" in Carlo Ginzburg, *The Cheese and the Worms. The Cosmos of a Sixteenth-Century Miller,* trans. John and Anne Tedeschi (Middlesex: Penguin Books, 1982), 95.

19. The growing power and expansion of the Ottoman Turks was a constant threat to Christian Europe throughout the fifteenth and sixteenth centuries.

20. It was a common Italian proverb to say that people who sang their own praises were forced to do so because they did not have neighbors or friends who would speak well of them.

21. Firenzuola is saying that if these women had read enough dialogues they would have realized that the narrative first person is not necessarily the author's voice.

22. See below, p. 9.

23. At the time the *Dialogues* were composed (1538), Firenzuola had re-entered the Vallambrosian order and was abbot of the monastery of San Salvatore.

24. Firenzuola is referring to Boccaccio's defense of himself and his work in the introduction to Day Four and then in the "Author's Conclusion" to the *Decameron*.

25. Firenzuola is subtly but clearly indicating that he does not adhere to the Bembian position on language and, therefore, will not seek to imitate the style and vocabulary of the two fourteenth-century writers Petrarch and Boccaccio. Pietro Bembo and his followers advocated a return to the vocabulary and style of Petrarch (for poetry) and Boccaccio (for prose). See, Introduction for a description of the "question of language."

26. Favorinus (fl. second century) was born at Arles and educated in Greek at Marseilles. A noted rhetorician, he moved to Rome and entered the circle of intellectuals at the imperial court.

27. Quintus Horatius Flaccus, known as Horace (65–68 BCE), was educated at Rome, attended university at Athens, and became a member of the intellectual circle patronized by Emperor Augustus. Horace was famous for his poetry, satires, and letters. In *The Art of Poetry* he discussed the importance of using current idioms instead of archaic words when writing (ll. 46–72).

28. Ital.: *San Giovanni a sedere* (St. John sitting down), was a popular expression for the old Florentine florin, a coin no longer in circulation, which showed St. John the Baptist sitting. The current florin, on the other hand, showed St. John standing.

29. There is no record of any such translation by Firenzuola, either printed or in manuscript copy. Perhaps the author is purposely misleading his critics.

30. The *First Version of the Animals' Discourses* (*Prima veste dei discorsi degli animali*, 1548).

31. Hercules, the most popular of the Greek heroes, was renowned for his strength and courage. Tradition credits him with performing Twelve Labors, most of which involved overcoming monsters.

32. A proverbial expression to indicate that, as long as he is alive, a strong man (lion) will not allow others to undermine him or make a fool of him (cut off his beard).

First Dialogue

1. An abbey in Prato, occupied at one time by the Vallambrosian monks. Today it houses the Collegio Cicognini.

2. Vannozzo Rocchi was the father of Clemenza and Selvaggia Rocchi, good friends of Firenzuola. The Rocchi were a noble family of Prato.

3. The image is drawn from the game of soccer, which has long been very popular in Italy.

4. We have retained the title Messer to indicate a gentleman, a judge, a notary, or, more generally, a man who commands respect.

5. Celso is referring to the four humors or dispositions that were at the basis of Renaissance physiology: sanguine, choleric, melancholic, and phlegmatic. A balanced mix of the four humors would grant a person a healthy constitution and a well-balanced character. Similarly, persons with a compatible arrangement of humors would themselves be compatible.

6. Momus, who epitomized criticism, figures in many of Lucian's *Dialogues*. It was reported that the only fault he could find in Aphrodite was that her shoes squeaked and were thus annoying. See Philostratus, *Love Letters,* 37.

7. Stesichorus (632/39–556/53 BCE), was a Greek lyric poet who based his poems on a variety of epic sources. Plato reports that Stesichorus lost his sight when he wrote a poem that defamed Helen. After writing a second poem, asserting that Helen never sailed to Troy at all, his sight was restored. See Plato, *Phaedrus,* 243a.

8. In Neoplatonic thought, there is a strong link between physical and spiritual beauty, between an attractive body and a virtuous soul.

9. Celso is saying that, as Selvaggia will grow older, she will lose her youthful complexion and, by implication, will not be as ready to ignore or contradict his compliments.

10. Cicero makes the point that Nature placed the eyes, ears, and nose high on the upper part of the body to assist their functioning (*De natura deorum* II, 56). In this context he does not speak of beauty per se. See the discussion below (pp. 26–30) on the positioning and use of the eyes, nose, and ears.

11. Plato, *Symposium* 211b.

12. Homer, *The Iliad,* xx, 242.

13. Maharbal (fl. early 3rd century BCE) was one of Hannibal's generals during the Punic Wars. After the Carthaginian army won the Battle of Cannae (216 BCE), Maharbal urged Hannibal to march on Rome, but Hannibal wanted time to think about the suggestion. According to the Roman historian Livy, Maharbal then said, "In very truth the gods bestow not on the same man all their gifts; you know how to gain a victory, Hannibal, you know not how to use one." Livy, *Ab urbe condita libri,* bk. 22, ll. 2–6; see the translation by B. O. Foster, Loeb Classical Library (Cambridge: MA Harvard University Press, 1922), vol. 5, p. 369.

14. Zeuxis (fl. c. 400 BCE) was a celebrated Greek painter who introduced the use of highlights and color gradations in order to make his paintings more lifelike. Perhaps his most renowned work was the portrait of Helen, painted by using a number of models. The story of Zeuxis and his several models was a popular motif in Renaissance artistic theory. Leon Battista Alberti drew upon it in his treatise *De pictura* (see especially sections 55–56); *On Painting and On Sculpture,* trans. Cecil Grayson (London: Phaidon, 1972), 97–99.

15. Gian Giorgio Trissino (1478–1550) was a writer who frequented the papal courts of Leo X and Clement VII. His many literary works show the influence of Greek as well as Latin models. His *I ritratti* (Rome, 1524) was one of the earliest and is certainly, along with that of Firenzuola, whom he clearly influenced, one of the most comprehensive analyses of women's beauty written during the Renaissance. See Mary Rogers, "The Decorum of Women's Beauty."

16. Lucian of Samosata (120–180) was a Greek philosopher, rhetorician, and writer. He is most famous for his *Dialogues.* In *Essays in Portraiture,* written to

compliment Panthea, a favorite of the Emperor Verus, Lucian emulates Zeuxis in reverse and describes her beauty by synthesizing the features of various statues.

17. The *Tusculan Disputations* (*Tusculanae disputationes,* written in 45 BCE), is a collection of philosophical dialogues set at Cicero's villa at Tusculum, where he would retire from the tempestuous political life of the period.

18. Aristotle wrote that "to be beautiful, a living creature, and every whole made up of parts, must not only present a certain order in its arrangement of parts, but also be of a certain definite magnitude. Beauty is a matter of size and order." *De poetica,* in *The Works of Aristotle,* vol. 11, ed. W. D. Ross, trans. Ingram Bywater (Oxford: Clarendon Press, 1949), Bk. 7, 1450 b 35.

19. Marsilio Ficino (1433–1499) was one of the most important philosophers of the Renaissance and the head of the famous Florentine Academy, the preeminent center for Neoplatonic philosophy. Ficino translated many Greek philosophical texts into Latin and Italian and wrote commentaries on them. His *Commentary on Plato's Symposium* is a seminal work and one in which Ficino united the principles of Neoplatonism and Christianity.

20. In his *Prose della volgar lingua* (1525), Pietro Bembo had discounted Dante as a writer worthy of imitation on the grounds that his style, whether in Latin or in Italian, was too harsh, often base, and did not possess that classical grace, balance, and decorum that the Renaissance sought to attain. Firenzuola is led to compare Dante's *Convivium* to Plato's *Symposium* by the fact that both titles mean "banquet," the first in Latin and the second in Greek.

21. Plutarch, *The Life of Alexander,* IV.2–4.

22. Socrates is known primarily from his portrayal in Plato's philosophical dialogues. Plato describes how Socrates reached the conclusion "that he did not know" in *The Apology of Socrates,* 21d–23b.

23. Aristophanes (d. c. 385 BCE), the great Greek dramatist, is one of the participants at the banquet described in Plato's *Symposium*. His famous oration (*Symposium,* 189b–193) is paraphrased by Celso.

24. Pietro Bembo (1470–1547), author of *Gli Asolani* (1505), *Prose della volgar lingua* (1525), and a collection of Petrarchan poems (*Rime,* 1530), was considered an arbiter of linguistic taste and an authority on love theory. See the picture Castiglione draws of him in his *Book of the Courtier,* where he gives Bembo the final word in the discussion on love (Book 4, chs. 51–73).

25. Mercury is the Roman name for the Greek god Hermes, messenger of the gods, also associated with fertility. In the *Symposium* Plato reports that Zeus himself, not Mercury, did the cutting in half (190e).

26. Aesculapius (Asclepius, to the Greeks), was Apollo's son and the god of healing. It is probably on the basis of this that Firenzuola suggests it was Aesculapius who healed the wounds of the halved humans. Plato, on the other hand, attributes the task to Apollo himself (*Symposium,* 190e).

27. This etymology is pure fiction on the part of Celso/Firenzuola. The term "hermaphrodite" derives instead from Hermaphroditus, son of Hermes and Aphrodite, loved by the nymph Salmacis. When the gods answered Salmacis's prayers that they be joined into one body, "they were no longer two, nor such as to be called, one, woman, and one, man. They seemed neither, and yet both." Ovid, *Meta-*

morphoses, trans. F. J. Miller, Loeb Classical Library, 42 (Cambridge, MA: Harvard University Press, 1916) IV, 285–88.

28. The chaste love of Socrates for the young Athenian nobleman Alcibiades is mentioned in Plato's *Symposium* (219b–219e).

29. Homer describes the Greek hero Achilles' love for his comrade Patroclus in the *Iliad.* It is Achilles' grief and desire to avenge Patroclus's death that leads him to return to active service in the seige of Troy, an act that brings about both the death of the Trojan hero Hector and, ultimately, the victory of the Greeks over the Trojans.

30. The devotion of Nisus for Euryalus, two of Aeneas's companions in his journey to Italy, is mentioned by Virgil in the *Aeneid,* where he describes how Nisus died trying to avenge his friend's death.

31. The temple of Artemis was burned in 356 BCE, the same night Alexander the Great was born. The criminal act was perpetrated by a certain Herostratus, who had thus sought to immortalize his name. On finding him guilty, the Ephesians passed a decree condemning his name to eternal oblivion—a decree obviously ignored by the historian Theopompus of Chios, who recorded the act and the culprit. Firenzuola uses the incident, and purposely refrains from mentioning the culprit's name, in order to indicate that the names of unchaste lovers are to be condemned to oblivion more than that of the unmentionable Ephesian. Dante uses the same technique of silence in the *Inferno* when, discussing the uncommitted, he has Virgil say "Let us not speak of them, but look and pass on" (*Inferno* 3, 50).

32. Laudomia Forteguerra Petrucci was a contemporary poet. Some of her sonnets had just been published in the collection *Delle rime di molti nobilissimi ed eccellenti poeti nella lingua toscana* (Venice, 1547). Others were published a few years later in the collection *Rime diverse* edited by Ludovico Domenichi (Lucca, 1559). Originally from Pistoia, she married the Sienese Petrucci, and distinguished herself during the Florentine siege of that city by leading a band of women in the defense of the ramparts.

Margaret of Austria, the illegitimate daughter of the Emperor Charles V by a Portuguese woman, was first married to Alessandro de' Medici, Duke of Florence (assassinated in 1536), and then to Ottavio Farnese, Duke of Parma and Piacenza. A woman of great ability, she served her stepbrother, King Philip of Spain, as Governor of the Netherlands (1559–1567).

33. Sappho (b. c. 612 BCE), one of the most famous and skilled poets of Greek Antiquity, lived at Mytilene, on the island of Lesbos. Many of her poems celebrate her friendships with women. She may have been attached to a community of women and young girls dedicated to the goddess Aphrodite.

34. Cecilia Venetiana seems to have been a Roman courtesan. The 1526 Roman census lists a woman by this name as living in a section of the city common to prostitutes, but does not give her occupation. During his years in Rome Firenzuola came to know personally a number of courtesans, and so this reference may, in fact, be based upon his personal knowledge. See Jacqueline Murray, "Agnolo Firenzuola on Female Sexuality and Women's Equality," *Sixteenth Century Journal* 22:2 (1991): 210.

35. Alcestis was married to Admetus, king of Pherae, in Thessaly. At their

wedding feast Admetus neglected to sacrifice to the goddess Artemis and conse-quently had to forfeit his life unless he could find someone to die on his behalf. No one but his bride Alcestis stepped forward to take his place. Some versions of the myth have either Persephone, queen of the Underworld, return Alcestis to life, or Hercules rescue her from the Underworld.

36. The myth of Orpheus and Eurydice is one of the most enduring of love stories. When Eurydice died from being bitten by a poisonous snake, her husband Orpheus descended into the Underworld in order to try to bring her back to Earth. Pluto, lord of the Underworld, agreed to let Eurydice follow Orpheus back to Earth on condition that Orpheus not turn back to look at her until they had reached the surface. In most traditions Orpheus, on his journey back to Earth, failed to resist the power of his love for Eurydice and, glancing back to look at his beloved, saw her disappear, this time forever, into the recesses of Hades.

37. Firenzuola misidentifies Tiberius Sempronius Gracchus as Caius Grac-chus. Tiberius (c. 210–154 BCE) was an important Roman official and able governor. He married Cornelia, daughter of Scipio Africanus, and they had twelve children. According to Plutarch, Tiberius found a pair of snakes on his bed. Soothsayers advised him to kill one or the other of them—if he killed the male Tiberius would die, if the female then his wife Cornelia would die. Out of love for his wife Tiberius chose to kill the male snake. Shortly afterward, Tiberius died, leaving his wife Cornelia a widow with twelve children. Plutarch, *Lives of Tiberius and Caius Grac-chus,* I.1–3.

38. Celso's phrase *trista semenza* echoes Dante's references in the *Divine Com-edy* to the damned, whom he calls *anime triste* (*Inferno* 3:35 et passim), *mal seme* (*Inferno* 3:115 et passim), *mala sementa* (*Inferno* 23:123), etc. Although not officially recognized as a canonical example of fine style (see above n. 20), Dante's *Divine Comedy* was widely read and tacitly assimilated, so much so that unacknowledged borrowings such as the one above occur with great frequency in most Italian writers of the time.

39. This is a summary of Diotima's speech on love in Plato's *Symposium* (202d–212a). See also Bembo's discussion of love in Book IV of Castiglione's *Book of the Courtier.*

40. "Sia tu men bella, io sarò manco ardito." The verse is not from Petrarch. It is probably a tongue-in-cheek comment by Celso who, on this occasion at least, is unabashedly fabricating his authorities.

41. Ital.: *favola da veglia,* literally a story to be told on an evening watch, a nighttime story.

42. Aristophanes was renowned for his satire. Plato's characterization of him in the *Symposium* is an indication of the esteem in which he was held in ancient Athens, an evaluation perpetuated by Firenzuola's description of Aristophanes as a wise philosopher.

43. The source for this notion is found in Plato, *Timaeus,* 47a–c.

44. Celso is referring to Neoplatonic concept of the body as a prison from which the soul will be liberated at the moment of death.

45. Marcus Vitruvius Pollio (fl. 1st century BCE) was a Roman architect and engineer. He is best known for his treatise *The Ten Books on Architecture* (*De*

architectura), which had a significant influence on Renaissance theories of proportion and form. The theory of the proportion of the human body and its conceptualization within both a circle and a square originated with Vitruvius and was adopted by Renaissance writers and artists such as Leon Battista Alberti and Leonardo da Vinci. Firenzuola's proportion of nine heads to one body is more elongated than the proportion of eight to one recommended by Vitruvius.

46. The seven liberal arts were divided into the trivium (grammar, rhetoric, dialectic) and the quadrivium (arithmetic, geometry, music, and astronomy).

47. Rogers, "The Decorum of Women's Beauty," 66–67, suggests this elongation of the Vitruvian proportions of 8:1 may reflect the Mannerist influence of the period.

48. The Three Canals (Le Tre Gore) is a neighborhood in Prato.

49. A large square in Prato.

50. One of the great families in Prato.

51. Ital.: *Ogni bue non sa di lettera* is a proverb meaning one cannot be an expert in everything.

52. A balas is a spinel, a gem that resembles a ruby but is of less weight and hardness. A balas ruby is pink in color.

53. Ital.: *gli spiriti*. Firenzuola is referring to the Neoplatonic concept of the eyes as the window of the soul, the place where a person's emotions, virtues, and other such noncorporeal qualities reside.

54. This description of the usefulness of the eyes, and the following discussions of the nose and ears, are paraphrases of Cicero, *De natura deorum*, II, 56–57.

55. In Neoplatonic thought the circle is the perfect geometrical shape, a reflection of the universe and the divinity.

56. Celso may be playing with a sexual double entendre at this point; the word *lubrico* also means "lewd, indecent."

57. That is, human eyes have binocular vision, whereby both eyes focus simultaneously on the same object, thus allowing for depth perception. Human beings may be contrasted with some members of the animal kingdom whose two eyes see independently and, therefore, lack depth perception.

58. Renaissance physiology held that mucus was matter expurged from the brain. Andreas Vesalius (1514–1564), the Belgian anatomist and surgeon teaching at the University of Padua, claimed that phlegm from the brain descended through a channel, was distilled by a quadrate gland, and then flowed out of the palate and nostrils. See *The Epitome of Andreas Vesalius,* trans. R. L. Lind (New York: Macmillan, 1949), 68. In his 1552–1555 treatise on good manners, Della Casa advises his readers: "And when you have blown your nose you should not open your handkerchief and look inside, as if pearls or rubies might have descended from your brain." *Galateo,* 7.

59. In the *Republic* Plato condemns laughter, forbids it among the Guardians, and says the gods should not be represented laughing (III, 388d–389a).

60. Amelia.

61. Verdespina's words do not indicate clearly the appropriate meaning; obviously everyone in the conversation understood her reference, but we are at a loss to rediscover it.

62. A church in Prato, at the time belonging to the Dominican order. Corpus Christi is a variable feast in late May or early June, celebrated in the Renaissance on the Thursday after Pentecost.

63. Celso seems to suggest that the beautiful Appollonia is somehow tied (that is, married or betrothed) to a man not worthy of her. Since we do not know who the historical Appollonia might have been, the reference is lost to us.

64. Cicero, *De natura deorum,* II, 57.

65. See above, n. 52.

66. According to Aristotle, common sense is that faculty of the soul that coordinates the information gathered by the five senses of hearing, touch, sight, sense, and smell. Aristotle, *De anima* III.1–2, 424b20–427a15.

67. This is possibly a reference to breasts containing both milk and blood. Rogers says the rosy nipples crowning the snowy mounds of the bosom are like spouts on a useful vase, designed to give nourishment to infants ("The Decorum of Women's Beauty," 67).

68. Celso considers the breasts not only beautiful but also useful containers because of the mother's milk that is in them. Celso is also playing with words, here, for the Italian word *robinuzzi* he uses to describe the nipples could mean both "spouts," because of the milk they give out, and "little rubies," because of their color.

69. See above, p. 29, where Selvaggia tells Amorrorisca to uncover. See also below, Second Dialogue, n. 50. Rogers suggests that Selvaggia may have allowed the veil to slip on purpose, to attract attention and flirt ("The Decorum of Women's Beauty," 70).

70. Aristotle, *De generatione animalium,* V.3, 781b30–785b14.

71. Apuleius, *The Golden Ass,* II, 8–10.

72. Celso is again fabricating his own folk etymology. *Leggiadria* derives from the Provençal *leujairia* (lightness) and not, as Celso would have it, from the Italian *legge* (law).

73. The Renaissance concepts of balance, composure, and studied but understated elegance are at the basis of this passage. See, for another example, Castiglione's discussion of *sprezzatura* (nonchalance) in *The Book of the Courtier,* bk. 1. ch. 26.

74. Selvaggia is again piqued by Celso's teasing, and responds with the thinly veiled jealous threat, "May God protect you if you do not tell us who she is."

75. We have no record of any woman by this name in Prato. Firenzuola seems to have created an amusing name that puns on Quadrabianca (White square or White squad?) and Buonvisa (Good face).

76. Selvaggia is quoting directly from Petrarch, *Canzoniere* 213, v. 1 "Grazia che a pochi il ciel largo destina."

77. The three Graces, or Charities, were daughters of Zeus. They personified charm, grace, and beauty, and were linked to Venus (Aphrodite). They were also associated with all that was beautiful and joyous, and often sang and danced at celebrations. Like the Muses, with whom they lived on Olympus, the Graces inspired music, poetry, and science.

78. Pausinias mentions the close relationship of the Graces and Aphrodite.

Although the Graces are not specifically identified as Aphrodite's servants, this may be inferred from their relative status—they were minor goddesses, whereas Aphrodite/Venus was one of the Olympians. Pausinias, *Description of Greece,* VI, xxiv, 7.

79. Aglaïa was the youngest of the Graces and was married to the god Hephaestus.

80. It is impossible to render into one English word the Italian term *vaghezza* so as to contain the three connotations mentioned by Firenzuola. We have opted for the English "charm" and beg the reader to keep in mind Firenzuola's first two meanings of "movement from place to place" and "desire."

81. *Riduci i pensier vaghi a miglior loco.* Petrarch, *Canzoniere,* 62, v. 13.

82. *Io son sì vago di mirar costei.* The verse is not in Petrarch's *Canzoniere.*

83. "Di quello che essi erano vaghi divenuti," *Elegia di madonna Fiammetta,* ed. Vincenzo Pernicone (Bari: Laterza, 1939), 10. The *Fiammetta,* written during Boccaccio's brief sojourn in Florence (1341–1344), is a prose elegy in which the narrator, Fiammetta, recounts how she fell in love and was then abandoned by her lover. The work is a well-wrought psychological novel set within the framework of late medieval thoughts on love and courtship. It is also the first Italian novel written in the feminine voice.

84. *Gl'atti vaghi e gli angelici costumi,* Petrarch, *Canzoniere,* 181, v. 13. Celso misquotes slightly, for Petrarch actually says "angelic words" (*angeliche parole*).

85. *Una turba di vaghe giovani,* Boccaccio, *Elegia di madonna Fiammetta,* ch. 1 (Bari: Laterza, 1939), 17.

86. Celso is punning on the name of the city; *prato* means "field." The flowers would then refer to the beautiful ladies of Prato.

87. The original *chi la spiana la guasta* is proverbial for the idea that the more one explains the details, the more one ruins the effect of the whole.

88. Venus. The etymology Celso is proposing is based on the supposed derivation of *venustà* from *Venere* (Venus).

89. "For this reason" refers back to the mistaken opinion that *venustà* derives from Venus.

90. For a discussion and application of this concept, see Robert Hollander, *Boccaccio's Two Venuses* (New York: Columbia University Press, 1977).

91. Aristotle, *Nichomachean Ethics,* V.1, 1129a15.

92. *Ibid.,* 1129a21–23.

93. Antonomasia is a rhetorical device whereby the general term is used in lieu of the specific name. For example, "the Queen" to mean "Elizabeth II."

94. The Chimera was a mythical animal "of divine stock, not of men, in the fore part of a lion, in the hinder a serpent, and in the midst a goat, breathing forth in terrible wise the might of blazing fire." Homer, *Iliad,* trans. A. T. Murray, Loeb Classical Library (Cambridge, MA: Harvard University Press, 1924), VI, 179–84. The Chimera came to represent a fantastic idea, an imaginary thing or an ideal that could never be realized.

95. Pozzonuovo is a street in Prato. Gemmula, who lived on that street, cannot be identified. The name is probably fictitious and puns on "gemmula," a small gem or pearl.

96. A square in Prato. The reference to the lady who lived there is lost to us.

The diamond was considered to be chief among precious stones, the hardest and most brilliant of minerals. In this passage Celso is suggesting that, by extention, the lady from San Francesco is of superior quality.

97. In fact, she was the wife of the tenant, Vannozzo Rocchi, since the garden was owned by the monks of the Badia.

Second Dialogue

1. In the First Dialogue Celso defines fair (*candido*) as a lustrous white akin to ivory and differentiates it from the less lustrous white of snow-white.

2. Petrarch, *Canzoniere* 160, v. 14.

3. Petrarch, *Canzoniere* 90, v. 1.

4. Blonde hair was the standard of beautiful hair in the Renaissance. See, for example, Botticelli's *Birth of Venus* or his *Primavera*. This is in accordance with Apuleius, *The Golden Ass;* see below, n. 12.

5. The reference is lost to us.

6. A cochineal is a small, bright red insect, similar to a mealybug. Its dessicated body was used to make red dye.

7. A street in Prato.

8. The *rosa alba incarnata* is popularly known by many names, including the Great Maiden's Blush Rose and the Nymph's Thigh.

9. Celso is again indulging himself in folk etymology.

10. See above, p. 15.

11. See above, p. 33.

12. Apuleius, *The Golden Ass,* II, 8–10.

13. Amorini were winged little boys, symbolic of love, such as Venus's son, Cupid.

14. In the beauty contest with Juno and Minerva, Venus was granted the prized golden apple of victory by Paris. See below, n. 63.

15. Vulcan (Hephaestus, to the Greeks), was the god of fire and the smith, married to Aphrodite. Apuleius does not discuss his qualities as a husband or lover.

16. This is a close paraphrase of Apuleius, *The Golden Ass,* II, 9–10.

17. Dion Cocceianus, also known as Dion Crysostom (c. 40–post 112), was a Greek orator and philosopher who spent many years as a wandering Stoic teacher. Among his students were Favorinus (see Proem, n. 26). His works include more than seventy-five speeches and a history of Rome.

18. Traditionally, Lycurgus is identified as the founder of the Spartan state and its strict legal and social organization.

19. In 480 BCE Leonidas, King of Sparta, along with 300 Spartan soldiers, held the pass at Thermopylae for two days against the numerically superior Persian invading army led by Xerxes. The Greeks were eventually outflanked by the Persians, who were guided through the pass by a traitor.

20. Actually, Homer generally describes Achilles as swift-footed. The references to Achilles' hair indicate that he was blond.

21. Apuleius, *The Golden Ass*, II, 8. Firenzuola is actually paraphrasing and summarizing Apuleius.

22. Bovinetta del Maleficio is not identifiable. Her name is probably a fabricated play on words ("pretty little cow of the evil eye") suggesting both an insult and a reference to her use of potions and lotions.

23. Bovinetta is covered in makeup like a floured fish ready to be fried.

24. Homer, *The Iliad*, I, 568, for example.

25. Jewels and gold. The Spanish river Tagus was believed to be gold-bearing.

26. A wooden figure used in jousting, often adorned with flowers. Usually, it represented a Saracen bearing a shield which knights on horseback were supposed to hit as they rode by.

27. A better, though not as precise, English rendering may be "chicory," which has long-stemmed blue flowers.

28. It is not easy to render into English the Italian wordplay in the names of the two flowers. As Firenzuola explains below, the first, *cappuccio,* plays on the word *capo* (head), while the second, *fioraliso,* plays on the word *viso* (face). This purely fortuitous coincidence allows Firenzuola to create, unabashedly, his own folk etymology for the names of these flowers. It is worth noting, parenthetically, that the English word "cabbage" does derive from the Old French *caboche* (head).

29. Politian, "Stanze per la giostra di M. Giuliano de' Medici," stanza 78, vv. 1–2, where he says "The virginal violet trembles, with eyes lowered, honest, and shy."

30. Clove-pinks are a European variety of carnation, widely cultivated for its clove-scented flowers.

31. Over-refined persons who find, or claim they find, even pleasant fragrances unpleasant.

32. The Italian original, *Mone Ciolle,* plays on the word *ciolla,* "foolish girl."

33. In ancient Greece, the Sophists were paid philosophers who taught any or all of the higher subjects of education. Because they accepted a fee for their teaching, they were much despised by philosophers such as Plato and Aristotle. By the sixteenth century, the term Sophist was applied to thinkers willing to avail themselves of wrong information in order to win their argument, or to anyone who, in an argument, placed the emphasis on form rather than content.

34. See above, p. 24.

35. Celso is probably referring to the Chapel of the Holy Girdle (*Sacro Cingolo*) in the Duomo of Prato. One should not be surprised that young people gazed at each other at church—Petrarch himself tells how he fell in love with Laura when he saw her at the church service on Good Friday, 6 April 1327. Thus, in a society deeply rooted in Christian religious practices, and quite unwilling to allow young unmarried women out of their parents' house unless it were to go to church, church afforded one of the few opportunities for young unmarried men and women to mix and interact.

36. Traditionally Juno is remarkable for her eyes. This reference to her nose remains elusive.

37. The modern equivalent might be "to keep one's nose clean."

38. It is not possible to identify the teacher. Celso is probably referring to some well-known bit of local gossip now lost to us.

39. That is, a nose whose tip turns down.

40. Brazil is a red dyewood, originally from the East. The modern country of Brazil was supposedly named after the wood, and not vice-versa.

41. See above, p. 30.

42. The verses are from Lorenzo de' Medici's mock love-poem "La Nencia di Barberino," (stanza 9, v. 3) in which the farmer-poet Vallera sings the beauties of the country-girl Nencia, his beloved.

43. The vital veins are the esophagus and the wind pipe, which carry the elements of life, food, and air into the stomach and lungs respectively.

44. Ital.: *un poco di fontanella, tutta piena di neve*. Firenzuola must mean not a fountain in the traditional sense, but the declivity of a spring.

45. Ital.: *soggolo*. Part of the wimple; the strap used to tie the wimple. By extension, then, that part of the neck where such a strap would pass.

46. The Adam's apple is part of the larynx at the front of the throat. Its name derives from the legend that, while eating the forbidden fruit, a piece stuck in Adam's throat.

47. Selvaggia's words are not to be taken at face value, for they are tinged with sarcasm. She is, as several times before, teasing Celso.

48. The Italian *animo* is difficult to translate, for it could mean both soul and spirit, as well as implying courage, strength, resolution, and so on.

49. Elizabeth Cropper provides a discussion of the tradition of the vase as an analogy of the female form, Firenzuola's use of this image, and its ultimate appropriation by Renaissance painters; see her article "On Beautiful Women," 380–81.

50. This echoes the Judgment of Paris (see Second Dialogue, n. 63), in which Aphrodite (Venus) may have won the contest by loosening her tunic and showing her breasts to Paris. It also echoes the discussion in the First Dialogue, where Selvaggia's veil slips off her bosom (see above, p. 31).

51. The reference is to religious plays performed at the church of San Felice in Piazza, Florence. The rosettes are probably the two curls at the top of the lyre.

52. Gleaners were a common sight in premodern agricultural communities. After the grain had been harvested, the poor were allowed into the field to "glean," or gather, the residual grain. Gleaning was limited to the old, poor, and infirm members of the community. Strangers and vagabonds were excluded. Gleaning was strictly governed by law, and was considered an act of charity.

53. Celso is being sarcastic at this point. Of all people, it is the husband who best ought to know whether a woman wears platform shoes.

54. In accordance with contemporary notions of modesty, Celso had promised to describe only those parts of the body that were visible in public, a promise that clearly excluded a discussion of the leg. Ultimately, however, Firenzuola's fascination with the female body overcame Celso's sense of decorum.

55. Thetis, a sea-nymph, was married to the mortal King Peleus. Their son was the great hero Achilles. Throughout the *Iliad* Homer characterizes Thetis as silver-footed (e.g., I.538).

56. Mona Raffaella is the protagonist of Alessandro Piccolomini's dramatic dialogue *Raphaela. Dialogue on the Beautiful Appearance of Women (Raffaella. Di-*

alogo de la bella creanza de le donne). Piccolomini was a member of the Sienese literary academy of the Intronati (the Enthroned).

57. See First Dialogue, n. 14.

58. Besides the flattery, Celso/Firenzuola is making the point that the present is better than the past. In fact, the Renaissance sought not merely to copy the Ancients, but to surpass them. Renaissance scholars, artists, and thinkers were interested in reviving the scholarship, art, and thought of the Ancients so as to be able to advance beyond them.

59. This is the statue of King Robert of Anjou which, until the end of the eighteenth century, stood at the entrance of the Palazzo Pretorio, or the Palazzo del Podestà, as Verdespina calls it.

60. The old woman is saying if her master liked her as much he would see to it that she was better, and more warmly, dressed.

61. See above, pp. 22–23.

62. Cacus, son of Vulcan, was a fire-breathing monster who terrified the countryside. He stole some of Geryon's cattle from the hero Hercules, who ultimately retrieved the cattle and killed the thief by twisting him into a knot and choking him. Virgil, *The Aeneid,* VIII, 190 ff.

63. Pallas Athena (Minerva, to the Romans) was the daughter of Zeus and goddess of war, hence, the reference to her arms, which would have been firm but feminine. The reference is to the famous Judgment of Paris, in which Paris, son of Priam, King of Troy, was to decide which of the three goddesses—Athena, Hera, or Aphrodite—was the most beautiful. Each goddess offered Paris a reward, and he chose Aphrodite, who had promised him the beautiful woman, Helen. Paris had been tending his father's flocks on the slopes of Mount Ida when he was commissioned to judge the three goddess's beauty, and hence he is called a shepherd, though he was a prince of the ruling house.

64. Three of the seven swellings (Latin: *monticuli,* "mounds") in the palm of the hand. In palmistry, each mound, or mountain, has a special positive or negative significance, depending on the circumstances. The mountain of Venus, on the ball of the thumb, is indicative of love and charity, or lust. The mountain of Jupiter, at the base of the index finger, indicates religiosity, love, and honor, or pride and ambition. The mountain of Mercury, at the base of the little finger, indicates love of knowledge, industry, aptitude for commerce, or dishonesty and love of gain. Celso omits the mountains of Saturn (at the base of the middle finger; wisdom, good fortune, or prudence), of the Sun (at the base of the ring finger; success, celebrity, audacity, or timidity), of Mars (above the mountain of Mercury; courage, resolution, or rashness), and of the Moon (above the line of the heart; sensitiveness, morality, or immorality and temper).

65. That is, the fingernails should not be dirty.

66. Celso is addressing Verdespina and playing on her name, which translates as "green thorn."

67. Pygmalion was a legendary king of Cyprus. He carved an ivory statue of a woman and fell so in love with it that he begged Aphrodite to bring it to life. The goddess agreed, and Pygmalion married the statue-woman.

68. Probably a reference to Firenzuola's madrigal (not an elegy) in praise of Selvaggia's bosom "Mentre che 'l mio desir con gli occhi appago." The mixed metaphor elegy/canvas is in the original.

69. That is, Celso is obliged to praise Selvaggia for being so aloof, but wishes she were not so.

Index

This book has been set in Linotron Galliard. Galliard was designed for Mergenthaler in 1978 by Matthew Carter. Galliard retains many of the features of a sixteenth-century typeface cut by Robert Granjon but has some modifications that give it a more contemporary look.

Printed on acid-free paper.